Roland Gustafson

D1179741

# GOD GOES TO GOLGOTHA

# GOD
## Goes to Golgotha

A Series of Lenten Sermons

*by*

W. A. POEHLER

*and*

W. F. BRUENING

1948

*Concordia Publishing House - Saint Louis*

# Table of Contents

*Little People of the Passion Story*

# The Man Who Lost an Ear

*Then Simon Peter, having a sword, drew it and
smote the high priest's servant and cut off his right
ear. The servant's name was Malchus. And Jesus answered and said: Suffer ye thus far. And He touched
his ear and healed him.*—JOHN 18:10-11; LUKE 22:5.

THE central person in the Passion story is Jesus Christ,
Son of God and Son of Mary. The central thought, or
fact, in the Passion story is Jesus' suffering and death on
Golgotha. The central purpose of the Passion is the Vicarious Atonement for the sins of the world. The central
symbol of the Passion story is the Cross.

Around this central point of the Passion story revolves
a great number of lesser figures and facts, purposes and
cross-purposes, plots and counterplots, in order to complete the drama of deliverance portrayed in the pages of
the Sacred Scriptures. There were Pontius Pilate and
Herod, the rulers who bandied Christ back and forth between them on Good Friday. There were Caiaphas and
Annas, the high priests who led the opposition against
Jesus. There were the well-known figures of Peter the
boastful, who denied Him, and Judas Iscariot, who betrayed Him, of John and Mary, who devotedly stood
beneath the Cross, watching His agony.

But in a farther removed and less distinct circle there were also some little people, less known, less important, like the satellites about the sun, who are also painted on the canvas of the crucifixion story as portrayed by the four Evangelists. I have chosen to call them "The Little People in the Passion Story." Included in these are the man whose ear Peter cut off in the Garden of Gethsemane, the man who fled naked from the Garden when Jesus was apprehended. Included also are the tragic figure of Pilate's wife, who warned Pilate not to condemn Jesus, the shame-faced Simon of Cyrene, who bore Jesus' Cross, the wailing women of Jerusalem, the murderous robber Barabbas, as well as the God-fearing centurion, who stood beneath the Cross and witnessed Jesus' death.

These are little people. They are of no particular importance in themselves, neither for their goodness nor their badness. They receive importance and are worthy of study only insofar as they throw additional light on the central person of the Passion story, our mutual Savior. For that purpose and with that end in view I invite you to join me as we search the Scriptures during these six weeks of Lent and contemplate the lives and the actions, the relationship to Jesus, and the utterances of these little people of the Passion story.

The first of these little people of the Passion story, whom I desire to present to you this evening, is Malchus,

## THE MAN WHO LOST AN EAR

I. *He was a servant who was called Malchus, a king*

II. *For him the King of Kings became a servant*

## I

Let us first review the incidents in the sacred narrative preceding the event described by our text. The time is Thursday of Holy Week, the week before Easter. After celebrating the Passover, a festival of the Jews, with His disciples in an Upper Room in the city of Jerusalem earlier in the evening, Jesus leads His disciples out toward the Mount of Olives into a garden, which has become familiar to us as the Garden of Gethsemane. Here He kneels down and prays for strength in the struggle against sin, death, hell, and Satan which is before Him. At the conclusion of the threefold prayer He returns to His sleeping disciples, Peter, James, and John, awakens them, and joins the remaining eight, who had been somewhat farther removed from the spot where Jesus prayed. It is at this point that the band of soldiers sent by Pontius Pilate on behest of Caiaphas, together with the servants and slaves of the high priest, arrive seeking the man whom Judas Iscariot, one of the Twelve, had agreed to betray to them. Judas performs his dastardly task. Jesus admits his identity and adds: If ye seek Me, let these go, thus gaining protection for His followers against the zeal of Caiaphas and the Sanhedrin. Peter, who only now first seems to realize what it is all about, asks: Shall we smite with the sword? And without waiting for Jesus to reply, he draws his weapon and seeks to kill one of the enemies. He succeeds, however, only in cutting off the right ear of the servant of the high priest. Jesus warns Peter to put up his sword, because no one, least of all Jesus, had asked him to defend his Master by force of arms. Jesus submits to capture. But before doing so, He performs a deed of mercy. He heals the wounded ear of the high priest's slave.

Who was this slave? Our text tells us that he was a slave belonging to the high priest's household. He was not a Roman slave, but a Jewish slave, as his name indicates. He had come along with the other servants and slaves of Caiaphas and the armed soldiers of Pontius Pilate to the Garden. As a slave he was not armed with a sword, but with a stave or club. A relative or kinsman of his was also in the group. They came together into the Garden, preceded by Judas. He is called a slave in the sacred narrative, not merely a servant. Servants and slaves among the Jews could be distinguished easily. The slave had his right ear pierced with an awl by his master (Ex. 21:6).

There was one more distinguishing mark which John reports in his account and that is the name of this slave. His name was Malchus, that is to say, King. Whether he had in his veins royal blood, there is no way of telling. Nor was the name Malchus an unusual one, except for a slave, one who did not even own the club he was carrying for his master, whose very body could be bought and sold as a piece of merchandise. For such an one to be called King was a paradox and mockery indeed. More than that, this slave and bondman with the ridiculous name of King, which perhaps was given to him in mockery, comes to grief in his service to Caiaphas. Without getting a chance to return a blow, he almost has his head split open. For doubtless Peter, the fisherman, was a strong man and intended to kill Malchus. Even though not killed, the slave suffered a mortal wound and would have bled to death if he had not received help from Jesus.

Now Malchus, this slave who was called king but whose name did not mean anything to him, is a picture of you and me and of the whole human race. We, too, descended from Adam as we are, were originally created for a higher destiny than is apparent in the world today. Man was created in the image of God to rule over creation, the fishes in the sea, the fowls in the air, and over every living thing. He was to be king. But by sin he became a slave, a slave to sin. He yielded his members to the service of sin, and they became members of unrighteousness. The Jews told Jesus, they were never in bondage to any man. That was false. Jesus says: He that serves sin is a slave of sin. More than that, the service of sin leads to death. The wages of sin is death. The soul that sinneth it shall die. Cursed be everyone that confirmeth not all the words of the Law to do them. As Malchus fell to the ground mortally wounded, bleeding to death, so the whole world lieth in wickedness, in sin, and in death. Caiaphas, the high priest, represented the Law; Malchus, the slave of the Law; his wounding, the death of everyone who seeks to gain life by serving the Law; the pierced right ear cut off, for it was the right ear as our text says, indicates the final end of those who are under the bondage of the Law.

We are accustomed to look to the Cross on Calvary and the suffering, dying Savior to see the enormity of our sins and the terrible punishment of them. But in this slave, whose name was Malchus, who lies bleeding on the ground, we see ourselves and what happens to us because of our service of sin. Except ye repent, ye shall all likewise perish.

## II

Left to himself, Malchus would doubtless have perished, because no one paid any attention to a slave in those days. But now let us note that our text tells us that to the servant who was called king there comes the King who becomes a servant. We read: "And Jesus answered and said, Suffer ye thus far. And He touched his ear, and healed him" (Luke 22:51).

Let us note first the statement of Jesus "Suffer ye thus far." He is not speaking to the slave, Malchus, as though at the moment He healed him He meant to say, That is enough of your suffering, now you are well again. Rather, Jesus is speaking to the group, both the group of the disciples who are about to engage in bloody combat in defense of their Master, as well as the servants and slaves of the high priest who have come to apprehend Jesus. To them He says, Cease, desist, stop your violence. Literally, Allow, or permit it to end!

Having thus caused Peter to return his sword to its sheath, having halted any further display of violence on the part of either the disciples or the slaves, having, in short, indicated His desire to submit to capture, to be bound, to become a bondman, Jesus steps to Malchus and touches his wounded head and heals him.

What a beautiful, touching picture of healing, compassionate mercy! The King of kings becomes a servant to perform an act of love and mercy upon a servant whose name was King. He beheld Malchus suffering, bleeding, sore-wounded, and dying and came near to him and healed him.

That which Jesus did for Malchus, He is willing to do for us and the whole world, to heal the wounds caused by the bloody and painful results of sin. The world in which we live has suffered a terrible wound from its service of sin. Europe writhes in its anguish as an aftermath of war. Asia and the Far East is starving. Hungry children look up and are not fed. Medicine, food, shelter, clothing, are needed. That is the outward wound of civilization. Inwardly is the corroding, festering, putrid wound of hatred, greed, envy, revenge, defiance, lust, murder, and retaliation. Like the wounded animal which bites the wound and thus makes it worse, so civilized man can only harm himself in his misery. Jesus says: Suffer ye thus far, cease and desist from the use of the sword to heal the ills of mankind, either to assure the existence of a churchly crusade by force of arms, or to oppose any religion by force. "And He touched his ear and healed him." Thus Jesus touches us and our lives and heals the wounds caused by sin. It is the forgiving, healing, soothing, calming touch of Jesus' hand on our hurt that revives, refreshes us, gives us new life. "I passed by thee and saw thee polluted in thine own blood, I said unto thee when thou wast in thy blood, Live; yea, I said unto thee when thou wast in thy blood, Live" (Ezek. 16:6).

This is the end of the account in the text chosen for meditation. We do not know what happened to Malchus after Jesus healed him. Did he continue to line up in the ranks of the enemies of Jesus or did he become a follower of Christ? We can only draw our conclusion in the form of a deduction gained from the picture drawn by the sacred writer of the inner courtyard of the palace of the high priest, Caiaphas, where Peter stands in the circle of light with the servants and slaves of the high priest, awaiting the outcome of the trial of his Master. A man steps up to Peter and says: "Did not I see thee in the Garden with Him?" (John 18:26.) The inspired Evangelist John describes this man as being a kinsman of the man whose ear Peter had cut off. And we ask the question: Was Malchus there? If he had been there, would he not have identified Peter himself? We believe that Malchus was not there. That rather he became one of Jesus' disciples and a follower of Him who had mercy on him in the Garden.

Jesus has healed you, my friend; has saved your life and mine. Shall we return to the circle of Jesus' enemies? Shall we take part in persecuting the followers of Jesus? Dare we be found in compromising places where it is dangerous to our faith to join in the "warming of hands," at the fire of coals lighted in the palace, dedicated to service of sin? Nay, let us who, too, have been healed by Jesus' saving touch, who by faith in Jesus are assured of eternal life, renounce our old manner of living, make a clean break with the past, dedicate our lives to the service of Jesus, and courageously say with the hymnist:

> Jesus, I my cross have taken,
> All to leave and follow Thee;
> Destitute, despised, forsaken,
> Thou from hence my All shalt be.
> Perish every fond ambition,
> All I've sought or hoped or known;
> Yet how rich is my condition!
> God and heaven are still mine own. Amen.

# The Man Who Was Known to the High Priest

*And Simon Peter followed Jesus, and so did another disciple: that disciple was known unto the high priest, and went in with Jesus into the palace of the high priest. But Peter stood at the door without. Then went out that other disciple, which was known unto the high priest, and spake unto her that kept the door, and brought in Peter.*—JOHN 18:15-16.

WHEN Jesus was taken captive in Gethsemane, all the disciples forsook Him and fled. However, not for long did they flee. Knowing who had betrayed Jesus, knowing who had taken Him captive, they did not have to guess where Jesus was being taken. Particularly two of His disciples soon paused in their headlong flight in the darkness of the night and turned around and followed the light of the flickering torches of the soldiers and servants who led Jesus toward the palace of the high priest in Jerusalem. Where Judas was at this time, we do not know. Whether he, too, followed the Lord Jesus into the palace of the high priest is not known. What went on in his sin-darkened, remorse-smitten, despairing soul that night we can only conjecture. Let us leave the unlovely picture of the betrayer and rather follow these other two disciples as they catch up with the band which led Jesus

to the palace of Caiaphas in Jerusalem, albeit they
stayed at a safe distance under cover of darkness. We can
imagine them discussing in hushed whispers the situation
that had befallen their Master, the risk involved in going
into the palace that soon shut Jesus out of their sight.
They doubtless also realized the hopelessness of any attempt to free Jesus in view of the stern command which
He had given Peter to put away his sword and desist
from any further attempt to defend Jesus. The discussion
ends when the disciple, whose name is not mentioned in
our text or in any of the Gospels, but who doubtless is
John, for he is the only one who records this incident,
decides to enter the palace to reconnoiter and, as it were,
get the lay of the land, to see what is going on. He enters
the palace and soon returns and, since he knew the high
priest and the doorkeeper, gains permission also for Peter
to enter. While Peter takes his stand in the circle of
servants of the high priest around a charcoal fire, John
occupies himself elsewhere. What Peter did while waiting
in the open court of the palace of the high priest is well
known to those of you who attend these midweek Lenten
services year after year; how he thrice denied His Savior
and how the warning and compassionate look of the
Savior calls to remembrance Jesus' warning earlier in the
evening and how bitter tears of repentance indicate Peter's
sorrow and contrition at his rash denial. What is not so
well known is the position of John in the high priest's
palace in that night in which Jesus was betrayed. What
John did and did not do, what his relationship was to
Jesus and the high priest, and the lessons which we can
draw from this for our own life shall form the basis of
our meditation this evening as we consider:

### THE MAN WHO WAS KNOWN TO THE HIGH PRIEST

I. *His acquaintance with the high priest assured his own safety, but endangered the soul of his friend and fellow disciple Peter*

II. *His silence at the trial of Jesus before Caiaphas makes him equally as guilty as the open denial of Peter in the courtyard*

III. *His sin of omission and silent denial required the warning, compassionate, and forgiving look of the Savior equally as much as the sins of commission by Peter*

### I

Our text states twice in successive verses that John was known to the high priest, in order to make plain why he could get into the closely guarded palace of the high priest, but not Peter. It is interesting to ask, how it was that John, a Galilaean fisherman, was so well known in the high priestly palace. Although this cannot be substantiated, it is probable that John was the salesman for the fishing industry of the house of Zebedee on the Lake of Galilee. Fish being a common article of diet, particularly among the Jews as it is to this day, one can readily picture how John might have become acquainted with the household of Caiaphas through his business dealings. In course of time, his interest in Jesus of Nazareth and his discipleship must also have become known to those in Caiaphas' household. But since John neither defended nor excused himself for being a disciple of Jesus, and because his errands were purely business dealings, his occasional presence in the palace was permitted.

However, that which was perfectly legitimate for John

and did not endanger his personal faith, became a dangerous thing for Peter. Because of his standing in the household of the high priest, John goes out and gets permission for Peter to enter and through this action endangers the soul of his fellow disciple.

The first lesson that we can learn from the man who was known to the high priest is so apparent that it hardly needs to be stated. It is the warning against giving offense, of causing our brother to sin through such actions of ours which in themselves may not be sinful. Your business, even as John's business, may take you into the midst of Christ's enemies and opponents. You may be able to keep your faith intact, but how about your friend and fellow Christian? Can you vouch for him? Can you be sure that he will not deny his faith? "All things are lawful for me, but all things are not expedient," says Paul (1 Cor. 10:23). You and I may be able to keep our faith intact in the presence of many otherwise compromising situations. But what assurance have we that our brother or sister will not fall into sin and denial of their faith when we introduce them to these same situations?

Let us become specific for a moment. A young lady takes a nursing position at a Shrine Hospital, or a Masonic Home, or any other nursing home operated by an organization which cannot be classified as other than Christ-denying. That she can work there without compromising her faith, cannot be denied. But if through her intervention a fellow Christian takes a position there and the soul of that person is endangered, she certainly is doing exactly what John here did for Peter. Again, you may be employed by wholly godless and unchristian employers, whose avowed stand on religion is contrary to Christ. Certainly you must seriously consider whether you can recommend that your friend seek a position of employment there at the risk of losing his soul.

If for business reasons there may be some extenuation for your presence in the household of the enemies of Christ, certainly your choice of amusements and social acquaintances must be all the more careful lest your fellow disciples thrust their souls into danger because you happen to know the doorkeeper and the household of Caiaphas. Let us heed the warning example of John, the man who was known to the high priest.

## II

Having led Peter into the palace of the high priest, John parts from him. Just where he went is not stated in our text. It is very probable though that he either entered into the inner chamber of the high priest, or at least was within hearing distance of the trial before Caiaphas. The reason for this is that vv. 20-23, containing the initial investigation by Annas regarding Jesus' doctrine and disciples, Jesus' answer, and the slap in the face by the officer, are recorded only in John and are recorded so that they indicate that the writer must have seen the actions and heard the very words spoken. But picture to yourself the situation. While Jesus is being falsely accused, denounced, and insulted, John stands by and remains silent. Certainly the open-mouthed, vociferous triple denial of a Peter was no more shameful and sinful than this silent denial of John. He had a particular opportunity, because of his being permitted in the household of Caiaphas, to speak a word in defense of Jesus. He passes up the opportunity. He, to all intents and purposes, aligns himself with the

cause of the enemies through his silence. Surely the poet
has adequately portrayed this silence of John when he
says:

> Tell me, ye who hear Him groaning,
> Was there ever grief like His?
> Friends through fear His cause disowning,
> Foes insulting His distress;
> Many hands were raised to wound Him,
> None would interpose to save;
> But the deepest stroke that pierced Him
> Was the stroke that Justice gave.
>                     (*Lutheran Hymnal,* No. 153)

The position of John was pregnant with opportunity
for a great confession of Jesus or for a great denial. When
Queen Esther, the wife of Ahasuerus, found herself in
a similar position in the days of the Old Testament exile
of the Israelites, when the enemies of her people and of
her God threatened to wreak havoc and destruction on the
Jews and she wanted to keep silent, Mordecai, her uncle,
tells her: "Who knoweth whether thou art come to the
kingdom for such a time as this?" (Esther 4:14.) Esther
took her life in her hands and interceded for her people,
her religion, saying: "If I perish, I perish!" (4:15.) "Whosoever therefore shall confess Me before men, him will
I confess also before My Father which is in heaven," Jesus
had said to His disciples. "But whosoever shall deny Me
before men, him will I also deny before My Father which
is in heaven," He had warned (Matt. 10:32-33).

"Who knows whether thou art come to the kingdom
for such a time as this?" You and I, too, are in this world
for a purpose. We are often placed squarely before the
alternative of denying Christ by our silence or openly confessing Him. Is it not true that the temptation of following in the steps of Peter and openly and blasphemously

denying that we are Christians and disciples of Jesus is not nearly so great as the temptation of John, to remain silent while our Savior is being denounced, rejected, compromised, and condemned in this world? Of course, there is danger in opening your mouth, in season and out of season. You may feel, that's the pastor's job. True enough, those that are placed in positions of leadership have the greater responsibility of testifying and not remaining silent. But John is called here in our text, repeatedly, not the Apostle, not the writer of the fourth Gospel, but merely a disciple. Are you not a disciple? Indeed you are. Therefore, be warned by the example of John not to deny Jesus by your silence but to confess Him before men.

> Stand up! stand up for Jesus,
> Ye soldiers of the Cross!
> Lift high His royal banner,
> It must not suffer loss.
> From vict'ry unto vict'ry
> His army shall He lead
> Till ev'ry foe is vanquished
> And Christ is Lord indeed.
>
> (*Lutheran Hymnal*, No. 451)

### III

When Peter had denied Jesus for the third time, we are told in the sacred narrative of His Passion that Jesus passed by and bestowed upon His erring disciple a look of compassion and forgiveness which brought Peter to remembrance and repentance—and he went out and wept bitterly. No such comforting and reassuring incident is penned by the Evangelist John concerning his own silent denial of Jesus on that shameful Thursday night. Did John also behold Jesus passing by? There can be no doubt about it. He did. Did he also go out and weep bitterly over his sins of omission, his silent denial of Jesus, his cowardice, and his fearfulness? We do not know. But this we do know, that Jesus did bestow upon him a special act of love and compassion of reinstatement as His friend and beloved disciple. This happened the next day when in the third word from the Cross the blessed Savior looks upon John and commits unto his care His grief-stricken mother. "Behold thy mother." There is no doubt that John repented of his part in the scene in the palace of the high priest. The man who was known to the high priest was still known to the great High Priest who shed His blood as a sacrifice not only for the sins of Peter, but also for the sins of John.

Let us take comfort also from this searching of the Scriptures to glean all the lessons from the incident of the man who was known to the high priest. Matthew, Mark, and Luke relate that Peter repented, that Jesus had special concern about him and through a loving look brought him back to the Savior. John is silent. But that which neither Matthew, Mark, nor Luke record—his own part in the incident in the palace and what happened to him, John himself records—the silent denial, and the loving forgiveness through the third word on the Cross.

Let us, then, acknowledging our own often grievous sins of omission in denying the Savior by our silence, bow beneath that blessed Cross on Calvary with John and behold the blessed Savior's glance fixed also on us in full assurance of the forgiveness of all our sins with which we, too, crucified Him. Let us hear Him as He, whom we have all too often forsaken and denied, confessing us before His Father in heaven, pleading our forgiveness, says: Father, forgive them, for they know not what they do. Amen.

# The Woman Who Dreamed About Jesus

*When he was set down on the judgment seat, his
wife sent unto him, saying: Have thou nothing to do
with that just Man: for I have suffered many things
this day in a dream because of Him.*—MATT. 27:19.

IN EXAMINING the sacred narrative of the Passion of our
Lord and Savior, Jesus Christ, we note an almost infinite
variation in the manner in which the little people of the
Passion story are presented to us. In the case of Malchus,
the servant of the high priest, we are told not what he
did, or what he said, but what his name was and that he
had his ear cut off. In the case of the man who was known
to the high priest, we are told not what his name is or
what happened to him, or what he said, but what he did,
namely that he led Peter into the palace of the high priest.
In the case of the little person presented to us this evening, we are told neither her name nor what happened to
her, not what she did, but rather what she said. The incident recorded in our text is found only in Matthew. The
whole incident is described in one single verse. And yet
there is contained here such a poignantly beautiful, albeit
tragic, incident in the greater drama of the suffering
Savior, that we have sufficient cause to center our attention upon this character as we meditate on

## The Woman Who Dreamed About Jesus

*I. We note her great concern about Jesus*
*II. We note her fearless confession*
*III. We note the consequence of her confession*

### I

The name of the woman who dreamed about Jesus, according to legend, is Procla, or Claudia Procula. Most commonly she has been given the name of Claudia by Bible lovers. According to the Eastern Orthodox Church she became a devout Christian, so much so, that she has been made a saint. The day of the year in which she is honored is October 27. She was no doubt a Roman lady from Italy who had traveled with her husband, Pontius Pilate, from Rome to Jerusalem when he received the appointment of governor of Judea. Although at one time women were prohibited from accompanying their husbands into the Roman provinces, since the days of Augustus this ruling was relaxed. While living in Jerusalem, she became acquainted with the words and the works of Jesus of Nazareth. She may never have seen Him nor heard Him directly. But such was the influence of Jesus that even in the seclusion of the Praetorium of the governor words and incidents and acts of Jesus came to Claudia's attention. No doubt she made discreet inquiries from her Jewish maids about Him and had come to some very definite convictions regarding Him. This, then, is the woman who on the day on which Jesus was condemned to be crucified dreamed about Him.

We do not know what her dream was, and it is idle to speculate about the contents of the dream. Also, it is a known fact that dreams often vanish completely from the mind of the sleeper the moment he awakes. Whether that was the case with Claudia, is not known. One thing she did remember. It was a terrible dream. In that dream she had suffered many things. The dream was about this Man who was being tried before her husband, Pontius Pilate, the governor of Judea.

Nor is it necessary to infer that this was a special vision sent from God, as was the dream of Pharaoh or the dream of young Jacob at Bethel. Incidents similar to the one recorded in our text are found in secular history as well. Thus the night before Julius Caesar was murdered by the hands of his friends, his wife Calpurnia had a horrible dream in which she beheld a white marble statue of Caesar spurting blood and heard the cry "Murder him! Murder him!" Although it did disturb Caesar, it did not keep him from going to the Senate. In spite of his wife's entreaties, he held his rendezvous with death and the assassins' daggers.

There is, however, one fact that rests not upon conjecture, but upon evidence supported by our text and that is that Claudia was greatly concerned about Jesus. Modern psychologists and students of the mysteries of dreams tell us that many of our dreams are self-induced. That is, when we take our problems and worries to bed with us, we are apt to dream about them. Claudia could not have dreamed about Jesus without knowing something about Him. She would not have dreamed about Him, had she not been thinking about Him and had not her thoughts been of a disturbing, anxious nature. "I have suffered many things this day in a dream because of Him," she says to her husband.

Here, then, is a woman who dreamed about Jesus, primarily because she was greatly concerned about Him. She must have been concerned about herself. Are we concerned about Jesus? Are we greatly concerned about ourselves? Pilate didn't dream about Jesus. Nor did Herod, nor Caiaphas. I shall not ask you, my friend, whether you dream about Jesus. But I shall ask you whether you are concerned about Jesus. What is Jesus to you? Is He merely a casual acquaintance of whom you never think except when you happen to meet him on the street? or in the church? Is He like the storybook, the best seller, which you once read and then returned to the library? Is He like the neatly arranged and carefully dusted guest room in the house, which is never used by anyone of the family? Is He like the souvenirs that the veterans bring home from the war, the shrapnel, the sabers, the flags, the foreign coins, to be arrayed neatly in displays, or kept in boxes and in bags, to be dragged out for display purposes only, which once meant something in the past, but no longer hold an important place in your life? Or are you like Claudia, greatly concerned about Jesus? Even though you may not dream about Him, He is still constantly in your mind, in your daily life, in your thoughts, morning, noon, and night, in your business, in your pleasure, in your recreation, and in your toil. I pray God that Jesus is for you your greatest concern in life and in death, in good days and in bad, in sunshine and in rain. Pray God that with the Psalmist you say: "Whom have I in heaven but Thee? And there is none upon earth that I desire beside Thee. My flesh and my heart faileth; but God is the Strength of my heart and my Portion forever" (Ps. 73:25-26).

## II

The woman who dreamed about Jesus was not content to remain a dreamer. She became a doer. She made a courageous confession of her convictions at the most critical time in the history of the world, when the fate of all nations hung in the balance. She sent to Pontius Pilate and said: "Have thou nothing to do with that just Man."

Pilate had reviewed the evidence that the Jews had trumped up when they came to him early on that Good Friday morning, demanding the death of Jesus. He found Jesus innocent. Again they accused Him, stating that He was from Galilee. Pilate sent Him to Herod, who in mockery returned Him dressed in a gorgeous robe. Pilate bethought himself of another expedient to set Him free. He recalled that on this day it was his custom to release a prisoner as a gesture of good will toward the celebration of the annual Passover, which had begun the previous evening. He called from prison the most notable robber and murderer and seditionist in Judea and set him opposite the innocent Jesus of Nazareth and demanded which of the two they would that he release unto them. It is while thus seated on the judgment seat ready to free one of the two prisoners, awaiting the verdict of the crowd gathered before the Praetorium, that Claudia sends her message to him, warning him against condemning Jesus and confessing Him to be a just Man.

We note that in her confession she states two facts. The first is that Jesus is a just Man; not merely a man innocent of the crimes He was accused of, but a just Man; a Man in whom no fault can be found; a Man above reproach; a "righteous Man," as the original has it. Did she here indicate her own faith in Jesus' vicarious righteousness? Who knows? Her confession of Jesus' righteousness coupled with her warning, to beware of condemning Him, would seem to indicate that she accepted Him personally as more than an innocent man who was being persecuted by His enemies.

Coming from a woman, and a heathen woman at that, at a time when all the disciples of Jesus had forsaken Him, when Peter had denied Him, Judas betrayed Him, John silently disowned Him, this confession of Claudia stands out as a bright pinpoint of colorful light on the otherwise dark and sorrowful scene before Pilate on Good Friday. When the disciples cowardly flee and are silent, when every hand is turned against our Savior, a lone woman dares protest His condemnation, dares proclaim Him just and righteous and innocent, and dares utter a warning against her own husband, the governor, if He condemn Him.

What a tribute to womankind is this confession of the wife of the governor! How proud and grateful must you Christian women be to know that once when your Savior was arraigned before the highest courts in the land, falsely accused, shamefully mistreated, crowned with thorns, beaten and abused, when all the brave men and courageous followers of Him turned their backs on Him and forsook Him, your sister in the flesh, a weak woman, had the courage to proclaim; "This is a just Man, let Him alone, have nothing to do with Him!"

You are sisters of Claudia after the flesh, are you not? You are Gentile women, not of Jewish extraction. You do know about Jesus, do you not? You do know that He is a righteous, a just Man. You know more than that. You

know that God made Him to be sin for us that we might
be made the righteousness of God in Him. Will you not
take Claudia for your example? Will you not, when all
about you are losing their heads, are denying, forsaking,
disowning Him, lift up your voice and confess Him? Will
you not take up the banner of the Cross and hold it aloft
for the world to see and confess Him in the words of the
hymnist:

> Jesus, Thy blood and righteousness
> My beauty are, my glorious dress;
> Midst flaming worlds, in these arrayed,
> With joy shall I lift up my head.

## III

Let us note finally what was accomplished by this
woman who dreamed about Jesus. At first glance we might
say, nothing was accomplished by her. Pilate condemned
Jesus in spite of her protest. She might have spared herself
the pains of seeking to influence the court. It was a hopeless situation. Only a fool would have sought to intervene
with the mob that gathered about the Praetorium steps
that morning. All that is true, but it is only a half-truth
at best. Pilate had indeed interviewed Jesus privately. He
had listened to Jesus' testimony. "What is truth!" was
his parting word, and he returned to the people out in
front. He might have excused himself later that he did
not know that Jesus was what He claimed to be; it was his
word against the accusers'. "What is truth!" God sent
him an answer from his closest and most intimate
acquaintance: This is a just Man. Have nothing to do
with Him. Yes, Claudia did accomplish something. She
fastened the guilt of condemning Jesus to death more certainly on Pilate, her husband, so that to all eternity he
will never be able to excuse himself.

More than that; by her testimony she fastened the guilt of Jesus' crucifixion more certainly on the mob before the judgment seat of Pilate. If she, a heathen, could discern the eternal verity that Jesus was a righteous Man and that divine vengeance would pursue those who ruthlessly denounced His claims, how much more should they have known! She left also them without excuse.

Still more, Claudia speaks to you and to me tonight. She is sending to us and stating: This Man is just and righteous. Do not condemn Him. Do not reject His claims. Do not turn your back upon Him. For the sake of your eternal peace and rest of soul and conscience, make your peace with Him, bow before Him and accept Him as what He is, your Savior.

Finally, Claudia here exemplifies the task of the Christian Church in the presence of the enemies of Christ. Ye are to be witnesses unto Me, said Jesus to His disciples. This Gospel shall be preached unto all nations for a testimony unto them.

Are you discouraged at the slow progress of the Gospel in this world? at the ignorance of the truths of the Christian religion among men? at the slowness of heart on the part of those who should know better but do not? Then realize that we, like Claudia, are called upon not to convert, not to win, not to change the destinies of nations, but to confess, to witness, to bear testimony that Jesus Christ is the Son of God. Pray God that you will bear that witness, in season and out of season, in the midst of friend and foe, lifting up your voice from the mountaintop, saying with Isaiah: O Juda, O Israel, O America, O World, behold your God! Amen.

# The Man Who Was the Choice of the People

*Now at that feast he released unto them one prisoner, whomsoever they desired. And there was one named Barabbas, which lay bound with them that had made insurrection with him, who had committed murder in the insurrection. And the multitude crying aloud began to desire him to do as he had ever done unto them. But Pilate answered them, saying: Will ye that I release unto you the King of the Jews? For he knew that the chief priests had delivered Him for envy. But the chief priests moved the people that he should rather release Barabbas unto them. And Pilate answered and said again unto them: What will ye, then, that I shall do unto Him whom ye call the King of the Jews? And they cried out again: Crucify Him! Then Pilate said unto them: Why, what evil hath He done? And they cried out the more exceedingly: Crucify Him.—MARK 15:6-14.*

*When Pilate saw that he could prevail nothing, but that rather a tumult was made, he took water and washed his hands before the multitude, saying: I am innocent of the blood of this just person: see ye to it. Then answered all the people and said: His blood be on us and on our children! Then released he Barabbas unto them: and when he had scourged Jesus, he delivered Him to be crucified.—MATT. 27:24-26.*

*Vox populi est vox Dei.* The voice of the people is the voice of God. This is not only an old Latin proverb, but also the guiding principle of a free people. We live and are ruled by majority vote. Our governors, legislators, presidents, and leaders are chosen by popular vote. The basic belief is that in a given question, the truth, or the right, or the better way, lies with the will of the majority. "The majority is always right" is a political axiom. That the majority is not always right can easily be shown. Many a scoundrel has been elected to political office. Many a good law or ordinance has been defeated, and many a bill which disregarded the real welfare of the people has been passed by a majority vote.

Now, it is true that in a democracy such as ours there is no other way than rule by the majority. Rule by the majority vote of the people is still a much better way of rule than by a dictatorship. The possibilities of the majority making a mistake, of choosing the wrong instead of the right, choosing their own disadvantage instead of their own good, are increased, however, when the people are ignorant and misinformed. It is the ignorant, uninformed mob that is guilty of lynching Negroes. It is the uninformed voter who elects the unworthy men and women to political office. It is the disinterested community that permits vice, crime, and violence to exist in its midst. The will of the majority must be directed by truth and a sincere desire for righteousness, or it will choose wrong.

How far ignorance, hatred, and misunderstanding can influence the will and the vote of the majority is set forth this evening as we examine another of the little people in the Passion story:

## The Man Who Was the Choice of the People

 *I. We note why the people choose Barabbas and reject Jesus*

 *II. We note the consequence of their choice*

### I

We are interested in Barabbas not for what he did in the Passion story, nor for what he said, nor for what anybody said to him, but merely because he was the people's choice over against Jesus of Nazareth. Who was this man? His name, Barabbas, means son of the father, or son of a Rabbi. He may have come from one of the cultured families of Judea. We are told he was an insurrectionist, a rebel. He had rebelled against the Roman yoke. He no doubt had gathered a group about himself, like Judas Maccabaeus 200 years earlier, and determined to rid the land of the hated Roman rule. He turned into a common outlaw, a robber, and a murderer. As such he had been thrown into jail with at least two others of his companions, as our text indicates. The death sentence hung over him. He was to be executed.

This is the man whom Pilate brings forth and sets opposite the Man who called himself King of the Jews and asks the people whom they wanted that he should release unto them. They had clamored that he should carry out the custom in Judea of releasing a prisoner to them on the feast of the Passover. But to the surprise of Pilate the people choose Barabbas and reject Jesus.

Let us examine the motives and purposes back of their choice. We read in our text: "But the chief priests moved the people, that he should rather release Barabbas unto them" (v. 11). How was it that the chief priests of the people could persuade a whole group of people to ask for Barabbas and reject Jesus? To understand this, we must remember that Barabbas was not all villain. Remember that he was a leader of an insurrectionist group. He had opposed the Roman rule. It was only necessary for the priests to inform the people that Barabbas had opposed the Roman rule, whereas Jesus had told the people to pay their taxes. That the leaders were contradicting their own statements and their own arguments before Pilate, was not detected by the people. Jesus they had accused of claiming to be a king and seeking to usurp the authority of the Roman emperor and refusing to pay tribute to Caesar, and they wanted Him to be prosecuted because He wanted to be king. Barabbas they want freed because he opposed Roman rule. But the people follow their leaders, and they are easily misled. All Jesus' teachings of humility, submission, the Kingdom of God, are lost in the vision of a kingdom of God on earth, in the Jewish Millennium of the return of the rule of King David in Palestine. And they reject Jesus and choose Barabbas.

But why were the leaders opposed to Jesus? Did they really believe that Barabbas was preferable to Jesus? Yes, in their false and deluded understanding of the Prophets they believed that Jesus was opposed to their real welfare. They believed that when Messiah came, He would establish a kingdom on earth and drive the Romans from Jerusalem.

That which took place there before Pontius Pilate on Good Friday is a true picture of man since the fall of Adam. Left to himself, he will invariably reject His Savior and choose the evil. He will turn his back upon the

Son of God and choose Barabbas. Not viciously, but because he just does not know any better. For the natural man is spiritually blind, dead, and an enemy of God. When the cry arose that Friday morning before the court of Pilate "Crucify, crucify Him!" every voice of every human being that ever lived was mingled there. Our voices, too, were raised there.

> Ah, I also and my sin wrought Thy deep affliction.
> This indeed the cause hath been of Thy crucifixion.

And yet we cannot fail to bring in another thought. The choice of the people was not an accident. The rejection of Jesus was not a tragedy that could not have been prevented. God had not abdicated on Good Friday. God watched while mankind rejected their Christ and chose Barabbas. God knew from eternity that that was what would happen. Knew it, but did not decree it. Rather, His heart, breaking with love and pity for sinful, helpless, hopeless mankind which in their blindness rejected their Savior, determined to bring good out of evil, used this act of hatred-filled, fearful hearts of his creatures to carry out His plan of salvation. For God made Him to be sin for us who knew no sin, that we might be made the righteousness of God in Him. God laid on Him the iniquity of us all. God chose to permit Barabbas to be freed and Jesus, the holy, innocent One to be condemned—for our salvation. For Barabbas is we, Pilate represents God, the eternal Judge, and Jesus is the sacrificial Lamb slain for us sinners, through whom and through whose substitutionary atonement we the sinful ones, we the robbers, the murderers, the unrighteous ones, are pardoned and released and proclaimed innocent. Oh, thank God for His unspeakable mercy, who permitted His Son to be rejected by men, that His creatures might be pardoned! Oh, thank the blessed Savior for His willingness to bear the shame of being rejected and sentenced to the Cross in our stead, in the stead of Barabbas, and in the stead of every sinful son of man! Oh, thank God the Holy Spirit for granting us that saving knowledge that we behold here on Gabbatha, the court of Pilate, the drama of divine justice, which accredits us with the innocence of Jesus and proclaims us pardoned, redeemed, forgiven before the tribunal of God!

## II

But, alas, this consequence of the fateful choice of the people in demanding the release of Barabbas and the rejection and crucifixion of Jesus, which God earnestly desired, namely, the salvation of His people, is not an irresistible consequence. When Pilate stood helpless before the surprising decision of the people in their choice of Barabbas, he asks: "Why, what evil hath He done?" But they insist on Jesus being crucified. But before giving in to their will, Pilate performs a symbolic act. He cleanses his hands with water and proclaims himself innocent of the blood of Jesus. The people cry out that they are willing to take the consequence of putting Him to death: "His blood be on us and on our children!" That is to say, if Jesus is innocent, may God punish us for having put Him to death! So certain were they that their decision was just and right.

What poor, blinded, deluded creatures are these human beings, our fellow men! Don Quixote, the Spanish legendary hero, went about fighting windmills, thinking they were evil giants. Parson Adams in Fielding's novel goes about killing harmless sheep at night, thinking they are robbers and murderers. Here the people destroy Jesus, thinking He is their greatest enemy and asking God to hold them to account. It is the same Jesus who had healed their sick and comforted their poor and preached the Gospel unto them. He had not changed, but their eyes had been stricken with blindness. In striking at Him they had harmed themselves. In refusing His deliverance they thrust themselves into eternal bondage.

In a book by Oscar Wilde, *The Picture of Dorian Grey*, a young, handsome man has his picture painted. It is admired by all his friends as well as by himself. But the man falls into evil ways, into profligacy, drunkenness, murder. As he looks at his painting, he beholds the face and the features becoming coarse and vicious. Evil leers out from the eyes, the lines in the face betray dissipation, until it becomes the picture of a horrible monster. In hatred of the picture, Dorian Grey plunges a dagger through its heart and falls dead himself, pierced by his own dagger. The picture has never changed, it is still the same handsome youth. Thus God becomes a hateful monster to man when looked at through the eyes of sin. Thus even Jesus became an object of hatred and loathing to the people on that Good Friday. They sought to strike out at Him, to destroy Him—but what happened? Thirty-seven years later Jerusalem is in ruins. Their hope of a great kingdom of God on earth is destroyed forever. Their children vagabonds and wanderers upon the face of the earth.

That is still the consequence of making the wrong choice today. Blinded by erring human reason and sinful prejudice and pride, man still cries out: "Crucify, crucify!"

And in seeking to destroy Jesus he brings about his own destruction.

It is not as God wills, but in spite of God's earnest desire to save mankind.

Whenever Jesus becomes to you anything less than the beautiful Savior, the pleading, redeeming, forgiving, loving Savior, then ask yourself whether it is not you who are to blame. When you begin to turn your back upon Him, become proud and vain and determined to disregard God's Word and promises—remember the man who was the choice of the people and how horribly mistaken they were. When you are tempted to do evil and say: I will take the consequences of my rash acts, remember the Jewish people, who cried: "His blood be on us and on our children!"

May God grant unto us a deep understanding of our unworthiness and sinfulness and the sincere desire to behold in Jesus our only Savior for time and eternity. May God grant unto us His Holy Spirit that we choose not according to sin-blinded reason, but by faith, saying with the hymnist:

> My hope is built on nothing less
> Than Jesus' blood and righteousness.
> I dare not trust the sweetest frame,
> But wholly lean on Jesus' name.
> On Christ, the solid Rock, I stand,
> All other ground is sinking sand. Amen.

# The Man Who Bore the Cross for Jesus

*And they compel one Simon, a Cyrenian, who passed by, coming out of the country, the father of Alexander and Rufus, to bear His Cross.*—MARK 15:21.

AT THE time of the birth of Christ we are told of a governor of Syria by the name of Cyrenius, who, in accordance with the decree of Caesar Augustus at Rome, commanded all inhabitants of the Holy Land to repair to their native cities and villages to have their names written into lists for the purpose of taxation by the Roman Government. Through the instrumentality of this Governor of Syria, Cyrenius, God brought Joseph and Mary, who were of the house and lineage of David, to Bethlehem just at the time when Jesus, the promised Messiah and Savior, was to be born.

At the time of Jesus' death, when He was being led out to Calvary to be crucified, another man, whose name was not Cyrenius, but who came from the land of Cyrene, modern Tripoli in North Africa, happened to be just at the right place at the right time to render a service to Jesus, namely, to bear the Cross after Him up to Golgotha. The name of the man was Simon. He had two sons by the name of Alexander and Rufus. He was a

disciple of Jesus. His wife and his son Rufus are mentioned by Paul in Romans 16:13. He was a God-fearing
man who had come to Jerusalem from Cyrene to observe
the Passover. Like many other pilgrims, he had not found
lodging in the city and was compelled to make his abode
out in the country at night. This is the man who happened
to come to the city gates toward nine o'clock in the morning on that Good Friday almost twenty centuries ago, just
as they were leading Jesus and the two malefactors out
toward the place of crucifixion. Jesus had carried the
heavy beams of the Cross upon His back thus far, but at
the city gate the exhaustion of His body overcame Him
so that it became evident that He could not carry it
farther. The Roman soldiers, seeing Simon of Cyrene,
who could be distinguished by his foreign garb, press him
into service and make him carry the cursed tree after Jesus.

This is the event which is briefly described in our text
this evening, and I invite you to meditate with me on

## The Man Who Bore the Cross for Jesus

### I

Let us note first why Simon of Cyrene bore the Cross
after Jesus and seek to learn some lessons on cross-bearing.

We read: "And they compel one Simon, a Cyrenian
. . . to bear His Cross."

Simon, the Cyrenian, did not bear the Cross of Jesus
voluntarily. He was compelled to bear it. He did not
want to. They made him do it. Here is the first lesson for
us to learn. Cross-bearing is not a voluntary or arbitrary
thing. We do not apply for the job. The world presses us
into service. Keep in mind, the cross is, for the world, even

as it was for these Roman soldiers and these Jews which followed Jesus, a symbol of shame.

The cross which you and I are to bear is thrust upon us by the world. Because the world sees in you something that reminds them of Christ, they will make you bear the cross. They will heap shame and ridicule upon you because you are a Christian. You do not volunteer for that service. They bring it to you. They will compel you to bear the cross.

In the Christian Church today there is much unwillingness to bear the cross which is thrust upon us and a desire rather to choose the type of cross we want to bear. That may seem strange to you, my friend. But is it not true? We would all be willing to give our very lifeblood for Jesus in defense of our faith, but how many will give up a few precious minutes from their accustomed luxuries and pleasures to identify themselves with Christ and His Church? We would all be willing to be a Dr. Livingstone in darkest Africa and to let a lion bite us for the sake of the cause, but how many are willing to face the roaring laughter of the world and false friends when called upon to bear witness to the truth? We all would have gladly done what Simon of Cyrene did, bear the heavy timber of the Cross to Golgotha, but how many are willing to bear the burden of Christ today in carrying their fair share of work and contributions to His cause?

I do not know what your cross is. Maybe it is some lowly underpaid position, because you refuse to become dishonest. Maybe it is an almost impossible task, such as bringing up children in the nurture and the admonition of the Lord in a day when most parents are little concerned about the Lord and less about bringing up children. Maybe the cross that the world compels you to bear is your conviction that it is possible for you, a young man or a young lady, to enter the estate of holy matrimony with the determination that yours shall not be a trial marriage, a convenient arrangement, subject to divorce procedure under the slightest pretext, but for the purpose of establishing a Christian home. Maybe your cross is a family that claims to be Christian but lives like heathen, and your task is to live the life of a Christian in surroundings that have become completely worldly and hypocritical. But whatever your cross is, it has been placed upon you. You will cast it off and refuse to bear it at the risk of your salvation. Nor will it be too heavy for you. Jesus will be there to help you. "God is faithful, who will not suffer you to be tempted above that ye are able, but will with the temptation also make a way to escape, that ye may be able to bear it" (I Cor. 10:13).

Although Simon was compelled to bear the Cross, let us note that once the heavy burden was placed on his back, he bore it after Jesus. It was not his own, but Jesus' Cross, which he bore. There is a difference, isn't there? Peter says: "Let none of you suffer . . . as an evildoer" (I Pet. 4:15). If the drunkard develops cirrhosis of the liver and dementia tremens, he is not bearing Jesus' Cross, but the consequence of his own sins. If the murderer faces execution, he is not bearing Jesus' Cross, but his own sins. Let us note these lessons, then, from Simon of Cyrene, whom they compelled to bear Jesus' Cross. We bear the cross because the world thrusts it upon us, and we bear it after Jesus. It is His Cross.

## II

Simon of Cyrene bore the Cross after Jesus only up to Golgotha. Then he laid it down. It was Jesus that was crucified, not Simon. That is such a simple truth that one wonders that people need to be told this. But, nevertheless, we must impress it upon our minds often. Simon could not gain the forgiveness of his sins by his cross-bearing. When he finished the bearing of the Cross, the great Cross-bearer was affixed to its beams and took up the burden which Simon could never carry, the sins of the world, and atoned for them.

Your cross-bearing and my cross-bearing can never be sacrificial. It must always be after Him and for Him. Our cross-bearing may and should bring us closer to Calvary, closer to Jesus, as the hymnist sings:

"Nearer, my God, to Thee, Nearer to Thee. E'en though it be a cross That raiseth me." But it can never substitute for Jesus' suffering and death. It does not gain the forgiveness of our sins. We do not carry it to heaven. We lay it down at Calvary. Yes, we lay it upon Jesus, the spotless Lamb of God, which taketh away the sin of the world (John 1:29).

## III

Which leads us to the concluding thought about Simon of Cyrene, who bore the Cross for Jesus. Why didn't Jesus bear the Cross to Golgotha? You answer; Because He was exhausted. True; but was He not the Son of God? Would the crucifixion have been called off if Simon had not carried the Cross after Jesus? Indeed not. As the other incidents in the Passion story were in fulfillment of prophecy and were symbolic, so also this incident of Simon bearing the Cross after Jesus contains a symbol. Jesus did not deserve the Cross. It was not His Cross. He was innocent. He only assumed the burden of the Cross for our sake. The Cross belonged to the whole human race which had brought this woe upon itself by its sins. Simon of Cyrene represents the world, groaning and burdened underneath the weight of sin, death, and condemnation. He carries it right up to Calvary, where Jesus assumes it to redeem the world. "God made Him to be sin for us who knew no sin, that we might be made the righteousness of God in Him" (II Cor. 5:21). "Surely He hath borne our griefs and carried our sorrows. Yet we did esteem Him stricken, smitten of God, and afflicted. But He was wounded for our transgressions; He was bruised for our iniquities. The chastisement of our peace was upon Him, and with His stripes we are healed." (Is. 53:4-5.) "Christ hath redeemed us from the curse of the Law, being made a curse for us; for it is written: Cursed is everyone that hangeth on a tree" (Gal. 3:13).

From Simon we learn *how* to bear the cross. From Calvary we learn *where* to lay it down. From Jesus, the great Cross-bearer, we learn that its curse has been changed by His suffering into a blessing, its bitterness through His sorrow into sweetness, its death by His substitutionary death into life, its shame through His bearing our shame into a symbol of glory.

May we never be ashamed of Jesus' Cross, for it is our symbol of life and hope. May we never despise to bear it after Him. May we proudly sing and say:

In the Cross of Christ I glory,
Tow'ring o'er the wrecks of time.
All the light of sacred story
Gathers round its head sublime.

Bane and blessing, pain and pleasure,
By the Cross are sanctified;
Peace is there that knows no measure,
Joys that through all time abide. Amen.

# The Woman Who Wept Over Jesus

*And there followed Him a great company of people, and of women which also bewailed and lamented Him. But Jesus, turning unto them, said: Daughters of Jerusalem, weep not for Me, but weep for yourselves and for your children. For, behold, the days are coming, in the which they shall say: Blessed are the barren and the wombs that never bare and the paps which never gave suck. Then shall they begin to say to the mountains: Fall on us; and to the hills: Cover us. For if they do these things in a green tree, what shall be done in the dry?—LUKE 23:27-31.*

AMONG the little people in the Passion story who help to make up the sacred narrative of our Lord's suffering and death is a group of women from Jerusalem who followed Him from the Judgment Hall of Pilate out through the city gates to Calvary, the Mount of Crucifixion. They are of interest to us because their weeping and lamenting over the condemned Jesus caused Him to utter the only words which He spoke between the time He was condemned and His crucifixion. After being relieved of the heavy Cross, which was placed by the soldiers on the back of Simon of Cyrene, Jesus turns to the weeping and lamenting women and says: "Daughters of Jerusalem, weep not for Me, but weep for yourselves." It is because these words were addressed to these women that they deserve our attention this evening. I present to you, then,

## The Women Who Wept Over Jesus

I. *Let us note why they wept*
II. *Let us note why they should have wept*

### I

We are not told the names of any of the women who followed Jesus out through the gates of the city toward Mount Calvary. It is quite probable that among them there must have been such as Mary Magdalene, and Mary the mother of Jesus, even as a Nicodemus, a John, a Joseph of Arimathea, doubtless were among the men. Nor can there be any doubt about it that these faithful followers of Jesus were sorrowful and downcast because of the suffering of their Lord and Master. In fact, we know that this hour of suffering sorrow had already been predicted for Mary by Simeon on the day of the presentation of Jesus in the Temple, when he said: "Yea, a sword shall pierce through thy own soul also" (Luke 2:35).

But it is not primarily to these that Jesus is speaking. He is speaking to a certain type, a certain class of women. He calls them "Daughters of Jerusalem," the feminine counterpart of the religion and politics, the hypocrisy, the hardness of heart of the men who dominated the city of Jerusalem. They are the women which Jerusalem, the heart of Israelitish teaching, had produced. They, like Jerusalem, had not hearkened to His teachings and His warnings and His love.

Their hardness, however, is not such that they can behold human suffering and agony without the utterance of a sigh and a groan. Their feminine heart gives way to tears. They still reflect the poet's description that "Men must work, and women must weep." Nor is Jesus rebuking them for their tears, as though He meant to imply that such a spectacle of weeping was unseemly and out of place. He Himself had wept at the tomb of Lazarus. He Himself, in the forepart of that fateful week, had wept over the city of Jerusalem.

Rather, He rebukes them because of the reason for which they wept. They wept because they beheld suffering and agony and did not inquire the reason for that suffering and agony. They did not realize that they, too, were the cause of the suffering and agony of Jesus. They forgot what their own Prophet Isaiah had said: "Surely He hath borne our griefs and carried our sorrows" (Is. 53:4). They believed that Jesus had been rejected by God. They forgot that God made Him who knew no sin to be sin for them.

Because they were moved by a false sense of mere pity, Jesus rebukes the daughters of Jerusalem and says: "Daughters of Jerusalem, weep not for Me."

Because men and women alike are still moved to tears and pity for Jesus when the Passion story is presented to them, the words of Jesus "Weep not for Me" must be repeated today. During the 13th century whole nations were moved to tears because they supposed that Jesus suffered because the Holy Land was in the possession of the Mohammedans. An undying hatred was developed in the minds of people against the Mohammedan Turks. Today the nations, the Christian nations, have joined this holy crusade against the Turk, not out of pity for Jesus, but out of love for rich oil lands.

You have the same theme developed in the hatred for

the Jews. They have been slaughtered like sheep, hanged like criminals, shot like dogs, by every Christian nation under the sun as a result of a false sense of pity for Jesus the crucified.

We bewail and lament the bombing of St. Paul's Cathedral in London, the destruction of the architectural beauties of Europe, the destruction of churches, schools, libraries, Christian literature, Christian pastors, and Christian people, but do we realize that we caused that destruction? that we went to war, that we hurled the bomb on Hiroshima and Nagasaki? Of course, the people of Europe are to be pitied and every endeavor fostered to succor their physical need, but the real lamenting should be over ourselves who took part in the horrible holocaust of the Second World War, over our and the people's sin, which is the cause of all wars.

While we are binding up the wounds of Europe and Asia, we are preparing the fuse to ignite the next war. It will not do to lament the consequences of war while refusing to recognize the cause, sin. It will not do to send mollifying ointment to the bruised and broken nations while refusing to recognize that you, too, have caused those bruises. Oh, yes, these women of Jerusalem had all chipped in to buy opiates for the condemned criminals, including the holy Jesus, to reduce their dying agony. But Jesus says; "Weep not for Me"—because they did not acknowledge their guilt in His death.

The picture of the compassionate, suffering, dying Savior should do more than move you to pity. If it does not move you to a repentant admission:

Ah, I also and my sin caused Thy deep affliction.
This, indeed, the cause hath been of Thy crucifixion-

then the Savior must say to you too: "Weep not for Me."

## II

"Weep for yourselves and for your children." Here Jesus tells them that they should weep for themselves. He elaborates and gives the reasons why they should weep for themselves. "For, behold, the days are coming in the which they shall say: Blessed are the barren and the wombs that never bare and the paps which never gave suck. Then shall they begin to say to the mountains: Fall on us; and to the hills: Cover us. For if they do these things in a green tree, what shall be done in the dry?"

The Savior is speaking of the immediate consequence of their rejection of His claims to the Messiahship. Their city would be destroyed. Countless numbers of them would die a horrible death. Their children would starve to death in their sight. Unspeakable anguish awaited them. Therefore they should weep for themselves and their own lot which awaited them because of their unbelief. Again, they could take an example from His suffering, for if that happened to Him, who was righteous, what punishment awaited the unrighteous and impenitent?

But neither Jerusalem nor the daughters of Jerusalem took Jesus' rebuke to heart. They did not weep over their sins. Thirty-seven years later the Roman armies came and destroyed their city. The mills of God grind slowly, but they grind exceedingly fine.

The Roman armies have long since crumbled in the dust. But the words of Jesus remain. They need to be stated most emphatically today. Daughters of Jerusalem, Daughters of America, weep for yourselves and for your children. Weep for the youth of the coming generation that certainly will be sacrificed to the devil of war unless there be heartfelt repentance, acknowledgment of our guilt, and a promise to live in the fear of God.

Christians can prevent war! Christians can turn the world upside down for Christ! Christians can stop the tramp of marching feet. But will they? Will you?

Lent will soon be over. Next week is Holy Week, with Communion services, crowded churches, overtaxed ministers and helpers, and the climax of Easter Sunday. Is that all that Lent means? Will next month find Christ forgotten and His message crowded out of the mind and the lives of His people?

May the picture of the Savior on the road to Calvary turning to the weeping women remain deeply engraven on your heart and soul. May His message "Weep not for Me, but weep for yourselves" fill our hearts with sincere contrition and repentance over our sins of omission and commission. May we turn to Jesus in true faith for forgiveness of all our sins. May we determine not to crucify Him anew with unholy living, but increase from day to day in righteousness and holiness of life, knowing on the one hand that there is joy in heaven over one sinner that repenteth, and that we are His workmanship, created in Him unto good works which God has before ordained that we should walk in them.

May we weep and lament when we look upon ourselves and our wretchedness, but may our tears turn to joy and laughter when we behold the blessed Savior who redeemed us that we might live.

May our prayer be:

Thou, ah! Thou, hast taken on Thee
Bond and stripes, a cruel rod;
Pain and scorn were heaped upon Thee,
O Thou sinless Son of God!
Thus didst Thou my soul deliver
From the bonds of sin forever.
Thousand, thousand thanks shall be,
Dearest Jesus, unto Thee. Amen.

# The Man Who Saw Jesus Die

*And when the centurion, which stood over against Him, saw that He so cried out and gave up the ghost, he said: Truly this Man was the Son of God.*—MARK 15:39.

ONCE more we come to God's house this Holy Week to meditate upon the Passion of our Lord and Savior, to confess our holy faith, and to draw strength and spiritual nourishment from the means of grace, the Word and the Sacrament. The events of this day customarily fill the churches of the Christian denominations throughout our land. As the various events in the life of our Savior did not happen in secret, but before the world, openly, so also the Church observes the commemoration of them publicly and openly. His birth, His suffering and death, His resurrection, His ascension into Heaven, His outpouring of the Holy Spirit on Pentecost were not secret, but were witnessed by multitudes. So also the commemoration of these events should be attended by multitudes of believing Christians. It is possible to observe Good Friday and Holy Week in the privacy of your home or in the retirement of a cloister or in a spiritual retreat. But the Christian, given the choice, will always prefer to confess his faith openly, in the presence of and together with other Christians and before the world. Even in that bitter hour

of darkness, when the Son of God died on the Cross sur-
rounded by His detractors and persecutors, the confession
of Jesus Christ, the Son of God, was not altogether
silenced. Even though the disciples had forsaken Him
and fled, though His own people had cried out: "Crucify!
Crucify!" though Pontius Pilate had, against better knowledge and conviction, condemned Him to the Cross, yet
God raised up a witness to His innocence and deity in the
very hour of His death. Who this man was, what he saw
and heard, and what he said shall form the basis of our
meditation on this Good Friday. I present to you:

### THE MAN WHO SAW JESUS DIE

### I

*We note first what the centurion saw*

The traditional name given the centurion, the officer
of the Roman guard to whom fell the job of carrying out
the crucifixion, is Longinus. Other legends state that he
was not of Italian parentage, but rather of Teutonic blood,
that he was one of those whom Caesar a century previously
had brought back to Rome and who, because of their
sturdy build and prowess with weapons, were forced into
service in the Roman army. Furthermore, that this Longinus later became a missionary to Northern Europe.
These and many other legends surround this character,
and we shall not enter into a discussion of them. Suffice
it to know that this centurion was an honorable officer of
the Roman army stationed at Jerusalem under the gover-
norship and authority of Pontius Pilate.

Of him we read that he stood squarely over against the
Cross of the crucified Savior and saw Him die. He was

there not by choice, but by command and in pursuit of his duty. He had watched Jesus, beaten and exhausted, fall beneath the Cross as he led Him out from Pontius Pilate through the city gates. He had seen the hatred and the enmity of the mob that followed Him. And now he saw Him nailed to the Cross, just another victim of the Roman law. But he had seen more. He saw the noonday sun covered with an unnatural darkness. He saw and felt the earth quaking beneath his feet. He beheld the rocks rending as if convulsed by internal agony at this horrible deed which outraged even nature. These things he saw, and being an honest, observant officer of the army, he took note of these things and pondered them.

## II

*Let us note secondly what the centurion heard*

The centurion also heard, says our text, Jesus cry out. He heard not merely the dying gasp of Jesus. He had heard much more than that. He had stood underneath the Cross from the beginning. He had heard this man pray for His enemies: "Father, forgive them, for they know not what they do." From other victims of crucifixion he had in his lifetime heard only horrible blasphemies and cursing vented upon their enemies. But here from the lips of this man he heard a prayer, "Father, forgive them, for they know not what they do."

He heard this Jesus of Nazareth expressing pity for one of the malefactors and assure him: "Verily I say unto thee: Today shalt thou be with Me in Paradise." Certainly this must have made a deep impression on the centurion.

Furthermore he had heard words of tender solicitude from the lips of this dying King of the Jews regarding His mother. He had heard with his own ears how this man, though dying, had nevertheless taken thought for the welfare and safety of His aged mother, saying: "Woman, behold thy son," when He commended her to the care of His friend and said to him, "Behold thy mother."

Again, in the midst of the awful darkness that lasted for three hours, he had heard the mysterious words issuing from this man's lips: "Eli, Eli, lama sabachthani?" He did not know what they meant, but the very tone of the words must have indicated to him somewhat of that forsakenness which the condemned victim felt in His innermost soul.

The last words from the Cross, "I thirst," "It is finished," "Father, into Thy hands I commend My spirit," were well understood by the centurion. Had he not sent a soldier to moisten the lips of the dying man with a sponge fastened to a reed and dipped in vinegarish wine? Had he not heard the loud expiring groan of the victim as He said: "It is finished," and again: "Father, into Thy hands I commend My spirit"?

Yes, the centurion was an observant man. He saw and heard the events of Good Friday out there on Calvary's hill. They were not according to his choosing, nor his desire. He knew that the crowd around the Cross hated Jesus. He knew that somewhere along the line justice had miscarried. He knew this was not a common man. He knew that this man claimed to be a king, the King of the Jews. He put it all together during those long six hours of waiting and watching for the end of the life of the victim of Jewish hatred, and the conclusion to which he came he did not keep to himself. He proclaimed it openly, publicly, fearlessly: "Truly this man was the Son of God."

## III

*Let us note, thirdly, what the man who saw Jesus die said*

We read: "When the centurion, which stood over against Him, saw that He so cried out and gave up the ghost, he said: Truly this Man was the Son of God." Did he mean what we mean when we confess that Jesus Christ is true God, begotten of the Father from all eternity and also true man, born of the Virgin Mary? Did he accept Jesus as his personal Savior? The full answer to these questions cannot be given. Certain it is that the centurion believed that Jesus was more than a mere man. Certain it is that he believed that He was unjustly condemned and crucified. Certain it is that he believed that God was offended and angry at the injustice done to this Jesus of Nazareth. Certain it is that he believed that this man had come to show His people the road back to God. Certain it is that Jesus had said of another Roman centurion that his faith was greater than any other He had found in Israel. We may certainly believe that this Roman officer who saw Jesus die was the first to give evidence of his personal faith in Jesus Christ, the Son of God, as his personal Savior.

And now I ask you, in the words of Jeremiah: "Is it nothing to you, all ye that pass by?" (Lam. 1:12.) Behold and see, whether there be any grief like unto that which ye see, any words like unto those which ye hear from the lips of the Crucified. "He was oppressed, and He was afflicted, yet He opened not His mouth. He is brought as a lamb to the slaughter, and as a sheep before her shearers is dumb, so He openeth not His mouth. Surely He hath borne our griefs and carried our sorrows. Yet we did esteem Him stricken, smitten of God, and afflicted. But He was wounded for our transgressions, He was bruised for our iniquities; the chastisement of our peace was upon Him, and with His stripes we are healed." (Is. 53.)

We have attended these Lenten services in which the whole Passion story of Jesus Christ was unfolded to us in song and prayer and Scripture reading and sermon. We have heard Him give unmistakable evidence to the claim that He is the very Son of God, the Savior of the world. Today we observe the anniversary of His death. What is your conviction, what is your confession? God grant that it be that of the man who saw Jesus die: "Truly this Man was the Son of God."

The centurion had no understanding as yet of Jesus' resurrection. He based his conviction on the evidence before him. We have more evidence. We can say: Truly this Man was and is and ever shall be the Son of God. We look from the Cross on Calvary to the open tomb of the resurrection, and add to our confession: He was delivered into death for our offenses, but was raised again for our justification. (Rom. 4:25.)

The same legend which tells us the name of the centurion, Longinus, tells us that this man was blind and that when he in accordance with Roman law made sure that Jesus was dead by thrusting his spear through His side, the blood that flowed forth from the wound flowed down the lance and touched his hand, which in turn, as he wiped his eyes, touched his eyes, and he received his sight. It is only a legend, but it has a beautiful application for us on Good Friday.

Our eyes, too, are blinded by our natural senses so that

we cannot see Jesus as our Savior. Our iniquities have separated between us and our God. His blood was shed to redeem us from our sins. And it is His body and blood which He gives us to eat and to drink in the Blessed Sacrament of His Last Supper to heal our sicknesses and diseases of sin. Let us, then, humbly acknowledging our sins, in true faith receive the assurance of His pardon and partake worthily of Holy Communion that our eyes may be open to the glory of His mercy, here in time and hereafter in eternity.

(*Lutheran Hymnal* No. 154; 1, 2, 3) Amen.

# What Think Ye of Christ?

*While the Pharisees were gathered together, Jesus asked them, saying: What think ye of Christ? Whose Son is He? They say unto Him: The Son of David. He saith unto them: How, then, doth David in Spirit call Him Lord, saying: The Lord said unto My Lord: Sit Thou on My right hand, till I make Thine enemies Thy footstool? If David, then, call Him Lord, how is He his son? And no man was able to answer Him a word, neither durst any man from that day forth ask Him any more questions.—MATT. 22:41-46.*

WHAT is the future of the atomic bomb? Will the United Nations succeed in maintaining the peace of the world? Will Russia one day fight America? Who will win in America in the present struggle between capital and labor? These are doubtless questions which affect directly or indirectly the well-being of everyone of us assembled here this noonday. They are questions which are being aired in the press and over the radio, in the magazines, and in the books of the day. However, important as these questions may be, I want to address a question to you which is a question of life and death, a question of supreme importance to everyone here today. It is a question which Christ Himself asked of the Pharisees and scribes and the Jewish people in the days of His flesh, shortly before His suffering and death. After working among them for three long years, healing their sick, raising the dead, opening the eyes of the blind, and preaching the Gospel to the poor, they still refused to accept Him as the Son of God and the promised Savior. He finally asked them the one important question which sooner or later everyone must answer. That is the question which I present to you today:

"WHAT THINK YE OF CHRIST, WHOSE SON IS HE?"

Let us note that Jesus answers this question Himself,

   I. *When He says that Christ is the Son of David and David's Lord*

  II. *Being the Son of David and the Son of God, He is the promised Messiah, or Christ, who was to come to save us from our sins*

## I

In Psalm 110, David wrote by inspiration of the Holy Ghost: "The Lord said unto My Lord: Sit Thou on My right hand, till I make Thine enemies Thy footstool." The blessed Savior quotes this text from the 110th Psalm and asks the question of the Pharisees and the scribes: If Christ is only the Son of David, how, then, does David call Him Lord, that is, God, his Creator, his Maker? And right there, my friends, we have a question which everyone must answer, not only those who joyfully and in faith accept Jesus Christ as the very Son of God, but also those who deny the deity of Christ and say that He was a mere man. If there is one thing that the sixty-six books of the Holy Bible agree on and repeat again and again, it is this that Jesus Christ, the Son of the Virgin Mary, is also our

God and Lord. Literally hundreds of Bible texts in the Old and in the New Testament bear this out. In the Old Testament, in Psalm 2, we read: "Thou art My Son, this day have I begotten Thee."

In the New Testament there is hardly a page which does not bear witness to the fact that Jesus Christ is God's Son. Thomas, eight days after Jesus' resurrection from the dead, beholds Him and says: "My Lord and my God!" Peter says: "Lord, Thou knowest all things." John says: "This is the true God and eternal Life." John, again, says in the third chapter of his Gospel: "God so loved the world that He gave His only-begotten Son, that whosoever believeth in Him should not perish but have everlasting life." The Apostle Paul confesses: "God was in Christ, reconciling the world unto Himself, not imputing their trespasses unto them." Jesus, arraigned before the highest tribunal of the Jews at Jerusalem, is placed under oath by the high priest Caiaphas and asked exactly this question which He proposes in our text. Caiaphas most solemnly asks Him: "I adjure Thee by the living God, that Thou tell us whether Thou be the Christ, the Son of God." And Jesus, under oath, on trial for His life, states: "Thou hast said, nevertheless I say unto you: Hereafter shall ye see the Son of Man sitting on the right hand of power and coming in the clouds of heaven." In answer to the question, then, proposed by Jesus Himself: "What think ye of Christ?" the Scriptures give an unerring answer: Son of David, indeed, but more, much more, Son of God, our Lord. Therefore we confess with the Holy Christian Church on earth in the Second Article of the Apostles' Creed: "I believe in Jesus Christ, God's only Son, our Lord." Therefore we accept the confession of

Dr. Martin Luther in the explanation of the Second Article: I believe that Jesus Christ, true God, begotten of the Father from eternity, and also true Man, born of the Virgin Mary, *is my Lord.*

## II

Let us note, why Jesus places this question before the Pharisees and the scribes. Why does He ask of them: What think ye of Christ? It is more than an academic question. It is more than idle curiosity. It is a question of life and death. "If ye believe not that I am He," says Jesus, "ye shall die in your sins." Oh, that the world would occupy itself, not with thoughts of inventing new atomic bombs, not with thoughts of producing airplanes that will go five, six, seven hundred, a thousand miles an hour through the air, but much rather with the answer to the question: "What think ye of Christ, whose Son is He?" in order that men might learn that in Him and through Him and by Him alone there is hope and life and an outlook for the future and salvation.

Last night the statement was made over the radio and in the press that there is in process of being discovered an atomic bomb which is much more horrible in its destructive power than the one that fell on Hiroshima and Nagasaki. This atomic bomb will do the destructive work of one million pounds of TNT. The imagination is staggered at the ruin and the destruction that can be hurled upon the world by the hand of man through the engine of destruction which his brain has conceived. However, that destruction is as nothing compared with the final inexorable fate that awaits those who refuse to accept Jesus Christ as the Son of God and the Son of Man who came to earth to save all men from their sins. As the threat of tramping, marching feet begins all over again in this sin-sick and sin-cursed world, let us, who are assembled here today, learn to our great joy and for our eternal happiness that Jesus Christ is the Son of God and the Son of Man, who has redeemed us from our sins. He alone holds the hope of the future and the key to our personal happiness as well as the happiness of the world. In the confusion that reigns round about us let us place the feet of our faith firmly upon this unmovable Rock and say:

> On Christ, the solid Rock, I stand,
> All other ground is sinking sand. Amen.

\*    \*    \*    \*    \*    \*    \*

*Invocation:*

Lord God, heavenly Father, who didst send Thine only-begotten Son into the world, not to condemn the world, but that the world through Him might be saved, grant by Thy almighty power that the forces of evil and hate, greed and lust, that are loose in this world, may be stopped and hindered, so that the Gospel of Thy grace and mercy may be brought to many who sit in the darkness of sin and unbelief.

O Lord Jesus Christ, Thou only Son of God and Son of Man, who didst shed Thy holy precious blood on the accursed tree in order to bring forgiveness of sins, reconciliation unto God, peace and happiness into this sin-sick world; we pray Thee, continue to have mercy and compassion upon mankind gone astray, that knows not the way back to God. Since Thou didst pray for Thy crucifiers on the Cross: "Father, forgive them, for they know not what they do," so we come to Thee, Thy trusting and redeemed children, praying Thee to forgive also our trespasses and the sins of the whole world, who are crucifying Thee anew with their sins.

O Holy Ghost, Thou only Comforter, we pray Thee, enlighten our hearts and the hearts of our fellow men that they may lift up their eyes from the fleeting things of this world and behold Him in whom alone we may find the road back to God.

O Thou blessed Trinity, God the Father, God the Son, and God the Holy Ghost, be with us this day in our noonday Lenten service, bless the preaching of the Gospel, open wide our hearts in true repentance and faith to receive Thy message, and grant us that wisdom which the world cannot know, and that peace of heart and mind which the world can neither give nor take away. Amen.

*Pictures of the Passion Story
from the Gospel According to St. John*

# The Arrest in the Garden

*When Jesus had spoken these words, He went forth with His disciples over the brook Cedron, where was a garden, into the which He entered, and His disciples. And Judas also, which betrayed Him, knew the place; for Jesus ofttimes resorted thither with His disciples. Judas, then, having received a band of men and officers from the chief priests and Pharisees, cometh thither with lanterns and torches and weapons. Jesus, therefore, knowing all things that should come upon Him, went forth and said unto them: Whom seek ye? They answered Him: Jesus of Nazareth. Jesus saith unto them: I am He. And Judas also, which betrayed Him, stood with them.*

*As soon, then, as He had said unto them: I am He, they went backward and fell to the ground. Then asked He them again: Whom seek ye? And they said: Jesus of Nazareth. Jesus answered: I have told you that I am He; if therefore ye seek Me, let these go their way, that the saying might be fulfilled which He spake: Of them which Thou gavest Me have I lost none. Then Simon Peter having a sword drew it and smote the high priest's servant and cut off his right ear. The servant's name was Malchus. Then said Jesus unto Peter: Put up thy sword into the sheath; the cup which My Father hath given Me, shall I not drink it? Then the band and the captain and officers of the Jews took Jesus and bound Him.*
—John 18:1-12.

Lent is a holy season. Every day is a holy day for the Christian, for each day is a sacred trust that God has given to him to be used to His glory. But this season is holy in the special sense that we set aside a definite time for meditation upon the suffering and death of our Lord.

On these Wednesday evenings we shall review the events of Christ's Passion and death. Our general theme will be "Pictures of the Passion from the Gospel According to St. John." The texts will be taken from that Gospel, beginning with the 18th chapter. Tonight we shall study verses 1-11, next week verses 12-27. We suggest that you study that portion before next Wednesday evening in preparation for the service. Read it several times until it becomes very familiar to you, and ask God's Holy Spirit for guidance and enlightenment.

Tonight's section from the Gospel of St. John takes us into the Garden of Gethsemane. John does not relate the story of Christ's agony in the Garden. However, though he omits the detailed account of it, he makes reference to it.

Jesus had spent Thursday evening with His disciples in the Upper Room celebrating the Passover. On that occasion He had instituted the Lord's Supper. He had held long conversations with them, warning them of the world's hatred that would descend upon them after He would leave them, giving them assurance, however, that He would continue to be with them. He told them that not only would He be *with* them, but would be *in* them, abiding in them, giving them spiritual life and power. He had prayed His beautiful intercessory prayer for them, recorded in Chapter 17 of St. John's Gospel. If you ever want to know *how* Jesus prays for you and me and *what*

He includes in His prayer, read that prayer again and again.

John tells us: "When Jesus had spoken these words, He went forth with His disciples over the brook Cedron, where was a garden"—and he adds that Judas knew the place; "for Jesus ofttimes resorted thither with His disciples." (vv. 1-2.) There are some who believe that Jesus and His disciples had slept out in the open in this Garden during the last week whenever He did not go out to Bethany and stay at the home of Mary and Martha.

His "agony in the Garden," as we call it—his great struggle in prayer was ended, and He arose from that struggle the Victor, prepared and ready to meet the ordeal ahead of Him. He had said to his sleep-weary disciples: "Rise, let us be going; behold, he is at hand that doth betray Me." He was ready to go out and meet His betrayer. We read in the account: "Jesus went forth" (v. 4), went out of the inner garden, went out to meet the group that had come to arrest Him.

In the events which followed we note the following characters who pass across the stage.

The first one who attracts our attention is Judas. John writes: "Judas, then, having received a band of men and officers from the chief priests and Pharisees, cometh thither with lanterns and torches and weapons" (v. 3). John writes as though the entire transaction were that of Judas. He indicates that Judas was at the head of the group. John does not tell us that Judas stepped out and kissed Jesus. The other Gospel writers had mentioned that John was the last of the four (Matthew, Mark, Luke, and John) to write, and so he often mentions the things the others omitted and often omits what the others had

recorded. John refers to the act of Judas in these words:
"Judas, which betrayed Him" (v. 2). Apparently Judas
had stepped out in front, kissed Jesus—for that was the
sign that had been agreed upon to indicate the man they
wanted—and then had stepped back again with the mob,
for John writes: "And Judas also, which betrayed Him,
stood with them" (v. 5).

What a tragic sentence that is! Judas was standing with
them. Judas, the former disciple, was standing with them,
the enemies of Christ! He who once had stood with the
disciples and enjoyed the fellowship of the Master, who
had listened to His teachings, was now on the side of the
enemies working against Him. He was standing with
them!

Such defection did not stop with Judas. Since that first
betrayal there have been many disciples of Jesus who have
enjoyed His fellowship and the fellowship of His disciples, who have learned His teachings and for a time
have walked with Him, who have then stepped over to
the other side, standing with His enemies. Many have
pledged their allegiance to the Savior at our altar at con-
firmation, many who at some time in their lives have given
themselves to the Savior, who have acknowledged Jesus
as their Lord, who in some time of great affliction have
made promises that they would turn over a new leaf or
who in a more calm and reflective state of mind have
determined to follow Christ. And then something has
come along which interfered, perhaps their marriage,
home, work, education, friends, social obligations, pleasures, or some other interest, and they have been swerved
from their purpose, have left Christ, have gone over to

the other side and now stand with His enemies. Such have betrayed their Savior.

Every time we do something which brings a blot upon the Savior's name or upon the Church of Christ or upon the faith we profess, we take our place with Judas, standing with the enemies of Christ.

Many people have the idea that they can follow a middle-of-the-road attitude, they want to be neither all out for Christ, nor do they want to be considered His enemies. But when Judas stopped being a disciple, he stood with Christ's enemies. Jesus says: "He that is not with Me is against Me" (Luke 11:23).

The final result of Judas' standing with Christ's enemies was that he stood alone. Lonely, desperate, rejected, and despised by the very ones whom he had befriended when he turned traitor, Judas, in despair, finally committed suicide. If we leave true fellowship with Christ and take our place with the world and the enemies of Christ, there comes a time when we, too, suddenly discover that we are standing alone. The world leaves us. The Christ we once knew has slipped away from us, the solace of prayer we once knew has been lost, the faith we once had has disappeared, the confidence we once enjoyed has vanished, and we, too, stand alone in despair. Judas is ever a warning to us as we see him, the former disciple, standing with enemies of Christ! Let us make certain that we are standing with Christ!

Another character who passes across the picture in the Garden is Peter. He had promised Jesus in the Upper Room: "Though all men shall be offended because of Thee, yet will I never be offended. Lord, I am ready to go with Thee, both into prison and to death" (Matt. 26:33;

Luke 22:33.) It seems as though he wanted to make good that promise, for when the band of soldiers came to bind Jesus, he felt called upon to do something about it. While someone asked: "Lord, shall we smite with the sword?" Peter had already drawn his sword and cut off the ear of one of the high priest's servants. We know from other accounts that Jesus healed the injury inflicted by Peter's blow.

Peter represents to us misguided zeal, zeal without knowledge. We often find a counterpart for that, too, in Christ's disciples and those who count themselves His disciples today. Fanatical zeal has at times done more harm than good. People have a distaste for fanaticism, whether it be in religion, politics, or any other sphere. Jesus disowned the rash deed of Peter. He must often disown the rash deeds of His followers. When a Christian is fired with zeal without knowledge, zeal without tact, he sometimes makes an approach to the unsaved or the indifferent that has little chance of being successful. The man who approaches any and every one he meets with the question "Are you saved?" may have a great missionary zeal, but does he accomplish his purpose? The Christian who approaches someone who doesn't go to church or who happens to be worldly with the assertion "You are going straight to hell," instead of showing the attractiveness of the Gospel and its blessings, may be testifying to the wrath of God, but he often brings only wrath down upon himself and saves no souls. Misguided zeal causes religious intolerance and bigotry. Misguided zeal has caused blood to be shed in the name of Christ. Misguided zeal has brought about vandalism against churches and synagogues. Misguided zeal is often the promoting influence for mobs and the rash things which they do. The way to prevent it is by serious reflection. If Peter had waited just long enough for the Lord's answer, he would not have been guilty of misguided zeal. If we pray and then wait for the Lord's answer before we act, we shall not be guilty of misguided zeal that does rash things, things which Christ must disown, as He had to disown Peter's rash deed.

Another group of characters that passes across the stage in the Garden was the multitude made up of Roman soldiers, Temple police, and some of the chief priests themselves. We note their utter helplessness in the face of the majesty of Christ. After Judas had kissed Jesus and then stepped over to the enemy multitude, Jesus stepped out with the direct question "Whom seek ye?" They answered: "Jesus of Nazareth." "I am He," He answered, and they fell back to the ground. This is proof that Jesus was not overwhelmed by force, but surrendered of His own free will. He said to Pilate: "Thou couldest have no power at all against Me except it were given thee from above" (John 19:11). Here is proof of that fact. He had said: "No man taketh My life from Me. I lay it down of Myself." (John 10:18.) Here is the proof of His assertion. Judas had betrayed Jesus with a kiss, but Jesus was not to be identified in this secret way. He openly confessed: "I have told you that I am He," in other words, I am the man you are looking for. And they could not lay hands on Him until He gave them permission, in fact, gave them the order and added: "If therefore ye seek Me, let these," the disciples, "go their way." (V. 8.)

We read they "bound" Him (v. 12). They had tried to bind Him before, but they could not. They had tried to take Him captive, but they did not succeed. Why was it that now they were able to bind Him? The only answer is that there was something else that bound Him besides the ropes of the police, and that something else was His love—His love for you and me. Not the ropes on His hands, but the eternal cords of divine love bound Him.

And this brings us to that person in the Garden who is in the center of the picture, Jesus Himself. As we mentioned, John says nothing about the agony in the Garden. But we see a reference to it in the words of Jesus which John records when Peter wanted to use force. Said Jesus: "The cup which My Father hath given Me, shall I not drink it?" (V. 11.) He had used similar words in His agony in the Garden. There He had made His decision. The Father had given Him a task to do, the tremendous task of saving the world. He must die for the sins of mankind. He must shed His blood, make atonement through the Cross. He must bring about reconciliation through His vicarious death and bring men back to God. Nothing would stop Him from that course.

You and I have our tasks—they are our tests. They belong to our Father's will. Shall we try to shirk them? Shall we try to be relieved of them? Or shall we not rather say with Jesus: "The cup which my Father hath given me"—whether it be the cup of sorrow, sadness, loneliness, sickness, trouble—"shall I not drink it?" We must say with Job (chap. 2:10): "Shall we receive good at the hand of God, and shall we not receive evil?" especially since we know that such so-called evil actually must work for good to us since we are God's own. So we see the resignation, submission, and determination of our Savior setting Himself to fulfill His Father's will, a will which included His death for our sins on the Cross.

We see His majesty in the power He held over His enemies when they fell to the ground. We see His tender love in His concern for the high priest's servant, whom Peter had hurt. We see His concern especially for His own when He insisted that they be let go. Even in the face of death the Good Shepherd is concerned about His sheep, that He might lose none. He has the same care and concern for us.

And so this first scene of the Passion history is before us—and as we glance now at the picture illustrating this story from the Bible, we note the characters we have seen this evening. There is Judas—alone with his money bag, for he has turned his back on Jesus, and the enemies no longer want him. In the left of the picture is Peter watching what is going on—with his hand still on the sword that symbolizes his rash deed. To the right in the picture we see the high priests who came along to make sure that all went their way, and in the middle of the picture are the soldiers who came to take Jesus captive. In the center is the Christ—bound by the cords held in the hands of the soldiers, but, more correctly, bound by the love that He had for you and me, bound by the love to His Father which drove Him on to finish His great work of redeeming mankind.

May the picture remind us, as we see forlorn Judas, to allow nothing to cause us to betray the Christ in word or action; as we see impetuous Peter, to think and pray and wait for God's answer before we do anything rash or impulsive; and as we behold the Christ, to thank Him for His willing submission to the will and plan of His Father in saving us and for His great love that binds Him so closely to us.

Lord Jesus, Thou art going forth
For me Thy life to offer,
For me, a sinner from my birth,
Who caused all Thou must suffer.
So be it, then, Thou Hope of men;
Thee I shall follow weeping,
Tears flowing free
Thy pain to see,
Watch o'er Thy sorrows keeping.

O Soul, attend thou and behold
The fruit of thy transgression!
My portion is the curse of old
And for man's sin My Passion.
Now comes the night Of sin's dread might,
Man's guilt I here am bearing.
Oh, weigh it, Soul;
I make thee whole,
No need now of despairing. Amen.

# Jesus Before Caiaphas

They led Him (Jesus) away to Annas first; for he was father-in-law to Caiaphas, which was the high priest that same year. Now Caiaphas was he which gave counsel to the Jews that it was expedient that one man should die for the people.

And Simon Peter followed Jesus, and so did another disciple; that disciple was known unto the high priest and went in with Jesus into the palace of the high priest. But Peter stood at the door without. Then went out that other disciple, which was known unto the high priest, and spake unto her that kept the door and brought in Peter. Then saith the damsel that kept the door unto Peter: Art not thou also one of this Man's disciples? He saith: I am not. And the servants and officers stood there, who had made a fire of coals, for it was cold; and they warmed themselves; and Peter stood with them and warmed himself.

The high priest then asked Jesus of His disciples and of His doctrine. Jesus answered him: I spake openly to the world; I ever taught in the synagog and in the Temple, whither the Jews always resort; and in secret have I said nothing. Why askest thou Me? Ask them which heard Me what I have said unto them; behold, they know what I said. And when He had thus spoken, one of the officers which stood by struck Jesus with the palm of his hand, saying: Answerest Thou the high priest so? Jesus answered him: If I *have spoken evil, bear witness of the evil; but if well, why smitest thou Me? Now Annas had sent Him bound unto Caiaphas, the high priest.*

*And Simon Peter stood and warmed himself. They said therefore unto him: Art not thou also one of His disciples? He denied it and said: I am not. One of the servants of the high priest, being his kinsman whose ear Peter cut off, saith: Did not I see thee in the garden with Him? Peter then denied again; and immediately the cock crew.—*JOHN 18:13-27.

TONIGHT's Lenten scene is the palace of the high priest. Let us note the characters in this evening's picture.

The first is Annas. There are really two characters introduced into the story at the beginning: "And they led Him away to Annas first; for he was father-in-law to Caiaphas, which was the high priest that same year" (v. 13).

The other Evangelists record the trial before Caiaphas. So John, supplementing them, records the arraignment also before Annas, which the others omit. It was merely of a preliminary nature and was not as important as the actual trial before Caiaphas.

This was the situation. Annas had been high priest from the year 6 A. D. to 15 A. D., having been appointed by the Roman governor. For some reason or other he was deposed, and his son was appointed in the year 15 A. D. Caiaphas, his son-in-law, was appointed some time later.

In judicial procedure there is often a preliminary hearing. So Caiaphas allows his father-in-law to conduct the preliminary hearing. Besides, it would take a while to call together the seventy-one elders of the Sanhedrin, or Jewish court. During that time Annas would have an opportunity to conduct this preliminary hearing.

John refers to Caiaphas, although he omits the actual trial before the Sanhedrin and Caiaphas. He reminds his readers that Caiaphas was the one who had declared at one time "that it was expedient that one man should die for the people" (v. 14). It was in their own interest that Jesus should be put out of the way. We today, in the perspective of time, see how right he was. It was to their interest, in a far higher sense, to our interest and the interest of every soul that one man, namely, Jesus, should die for the people, should take their place. This is the very center and purpose of our Lenten services that we review the events in the suffering and death of our Lord, not merely as historical events, but because we would see His suffering as our own, His death as our own, "one man for the people," for us. Christ died for us that we might live.

At the preliminary hearing Annas questioned Jesus concerning His disciples and His doctrine. His questions were not for information, but for the purpose of finding something which might be used to prefer a charge against Him. He was probably hoping that Jesus would declare Himself, reveal His disciples, and show how far they had been affected by His doctrine. He was looking for something upon which he could fasten a charge, something which would bring Christ within the jurisdiction of the ecclesiastical authorities, so they could then deal with Him. But he did not get very far.

Jesus answered in majesty: "I spake openly to the world; I ever taught in the synagog and in the Temple, whither the Jews always resort, and in secret have I said nothing. Why askest thou Me? Ask them which heard Me, what I have said unto them. Behold, they know what I said."

(Vv. 20-21.) There is an indication in Christ's answer of the contrast between Him and His accusers: He had spoken openly, He had done nothing in secret; they, on the other hand, had arrested Him secretly, they were holding His trial secretly. The candor in Christ's words caused one of the servants near by to strike him, saying (v. 22): "Answerest Thou the high priest so?" How dare you answer in that fashion! Jesus, making no reference to the manner of His answer but rather the matter of it, said in effect: "If it was wrong, prove it; if it was true, why do you smite Me?" (V. 23.)

That is all we know about the preliminary hearing before Annas. It accomplished nothing, and Annas sent Jesus bound to Caiaphas for the official trial.

Annas symbolizes the man who questions without really wanting to know the truth. There are people like that. They question our religion, they question the administration of the church, not in order to know, but to object, not to find out, but to find fault. Here is a person who says: "Why do you run to church every Sunday?" and even though we would tell him, he would not be convinced. He really implies: "I think you're foolish for doing so— I surely would not do it." By their very questions these people are voicing their objection. Others say: "Why is the church always asking for money?" They ask not to find out what the contributions are being used for, or what good such contributions are doing, or whether it is really true that the church is always asking for money. They are not asking us to learn something about God's requirements of Christian stewardship, but just to voice an objection, sometimes to provide an excuse for their own failure. When we ask questions, let us be sure that we really want to know, in order to act upon the information. Annas apparently asked merely to object.

The next two characters who pass across the stage of tonight's scene are Peter and John. In his writings John never names himself; so he writes: "Simon Peter followed Jesus, and so did another disciple" (v. 15a). That other disciple was John, the writer. "That disciple was known unto the high priest and went in with Jesus into the palace of the high priest. But Peter stood at the door without. Then went out that other disciple, which was known unto the high priest, and spake unto her that kept the door and brought in Peter." (Vv. 15b-16.)

Let us take a look at John first. He was known to the high priest. John is silent on the question how he had become acquainted with the high priest, and so we simply accept the record, he was known to Caiaphas. It was John who records the fact that the servant whose ear Peter had cut off had the name Malchus (v. 10). John knew that; the other Evangelists do not mention the name of the servant. John was so well known to Caiaphas that he could walk right into the palace.

Notice next how John admits a share in the blame for the defection and sin of Peter. It was he who went outside and spoke to the maid who kept the door and allowed Peter to come in. If he had not done that, John may have thought, perhaps Peter would not have fallen into sin. Not often do we find in people this trait that they are willing to share the blame for someone else's misdeeds. Usually it is the other way. They try to place the whole blame on the other party. Did you ever hear the report of an auto accident where the fault was not always that of the other driver? That is typical of our human nature.

How often are we really to blame for other people's faults and errors! When we see a friend or a member of our family err, before we immediately place all the blame on them, it might be well for us to take some blame ourselves. We may have contributed to their downfall, either by the things we have said or done or the things we failed to say or do. John shared the blame for the sin of Peter.

Next we turn our attention to Peter. We met him last week in a different role. He was the man of the rash act. Tonight we see him as the coward. Before we throw stones at Peter, let us not forget that one thing that prompted Peter all the way through was love for his Master. Love, indeed, coupled with curiosity, caused him to follow his Master into the high priest's palace and kept him close to Jesus, while others had fled.

It is interesting to read Psalm 1 in connection with Peter: "Blessed is the man that walketh not in the counsel of the ungodly nor standeth in the way of sinners nor sitteth in the seat of the scornful." Here was Peter walking into that counsel, standing at the fire with the sinners, sitting in the seat of the scornful, or scoffers.

Last week we heard these sad words of Judas: "And Judas stood with them." Tonight we hear the very same words about Peter: "And Peter stood with them and warmed himself" (v. 18). Judas stood with them because he had gone all the way over to them. Peter had not done that, but he was playing with fire when he stood by the fire and warmed himself.

If someone had met Peter at the door and said: "You had better be careful, Simon, the people in here are enemies; it's dangerous, you may get into trouble," he probably would have answered the same way that so many answer: "Don't worry, I can take care of myself." Many a person goes wrong because he thinks he can take care of himself.

Peter could not take care of himself. For the next characters who present themselves prove his undoing. The maid who kept the door said to him: "You are also one of this Man's disciples, aren't you?" The word "also" perhaps referred to the other disciple, John, who apparently was known to them as one of Christ's disciples. But he answered: "I am not." (V. 17.) I wonder how he tried to explain that lie, for people usually try to explain their lies to themselves. They never call them lies. They try to justify them. They make themselves believe it is much better under certain circumstances to tell an untruth than to tell the truth. Peter did not have too much of a chance to think about it, for along came the second temptation. Those around the fire asked this time: "Art not thou also one of His disciples?" and he denied again. (V. 25.) A short time later one of them said: "Surely you are one of this Man's disciples. You are a Galilean, and you have a Galilean accent," and another, a relative of the fellow who had received the blow from Peter's sword added: "By the way, did not I see you in the Garden with Him?" The other Evangelists tell us that he began to curse and swear. John does not mention that. And promptly Peter denied his Lord and Master the third time. We cannot read of Peter's fall without hearing the admonition of God's Word: "Let him that thinketh he standeth take heed lest he fall" (1 Cor. 10:12).

Suddenly something happened in the story which makes us forget Peter and think of Jesus: "Immediately the cock crew" (v. 27). A rooster in the early morning hour sounds his call, and though the narrative of John in this particular connection says nothing about Jesus, our thoughts go to Him as we remember His words of the night before: "Before the cock crow, thou shalt deny Me thrice." Another account tells us that the Lord turned and looked at Peter, and Peter remembered and went out and wept bitterly over his sin.

This probably occurred at the end of the night trial before Caiaphas as Jesus was being led away to safekeeping for the rest of the night until the morning trial.

It seems such a simple thing, the crowing of a rooster, and yet the Lord sometimes uses very simple things to call to mind His words, perhaps the chirping of a bird, the voice of a child, the report of some Sunday school lesson by a child, the ringing of a church bell, the hearing of a hymn on the radio, some picture. He sometimes uses these simple things to cause us "to remember the word of Jesus" and to turn us back to Him.

Many a person has been kept from some great temptation by the voice of conscience repeating a commandment he once learned or the voice of memory recalling the advice of a dear mother or father. God may be using this Lenten season as the cockcrow to remind us that we may have been keeping too much company with the wrong kind of people who do not know the Savior, sitting by the fire with them and warming ourselves.

We now turn to the picture. It does not portray all the characters that we find in this evening's section from John: Annas, who questioned without wanting to know, and Caiaphas are not shown, neither is John, who was probably inside the palace, who is willing to share the blame for Peter's sin. But there is the taunting maid, represent-

ing all those influences which would ridicule our faith
and tempt us to deny it. The soldiers, hostile to Peter,
represent those forces that are hostile to our faith and in
whose company there is every danger for us. There is the
fire which made Peter comfortable but proved his undoing; the cock up on the balcony in the left center,
Christ's reminder to Peter and a symbol of those reminders
that God sends us to call us back; Jesus, who did not give
up Peter, but with his look recalled him.

> In the hour of trial,
> Jesus, plead for me
> Lest by base denial
> I depart from Thee.
> When Thou see'st me waver,
> With a look recall
> Nor for fear or favor
> Suffer me to fall. Amen.

# Jesus Before Pilate

Then led they Jesus from Caiaphas unto the hall of judgment; and it was early; and they themselves went not into the judgment hall lest they should be defiled, but that they might eat the passover. Pilate then went out unto them and said: What accusation bring ye against this Man? They answered and said unto him: If He were not a malefactor, we would not have delivered Him up unto thee. Then said Pilate unto them: Take ye Him, and judge Him according to your law. The Jews therefore said unto him: It is not lawful for us to put any man to death—that the saying of Jesus might be fulfilled which He spake signifying what death He should die. Then Pilate entered into the judgment hall again and called Jesus and said unto Him: Art Thou the King of the Jews? Jesus answered him: Sayest thou this thing of thyself, or did others tell it thee of Me? Pilate answered: Am I a Jew? Thine own nation and the chief priests have delivered Thee unto me; what hast Thou done? Jesus answered: My kingdom is not of this world; if My kingdom were of this world, then would My servants fight that I should not be delivered to the Jews; but now is My kingdom not from hence. Pilate therefore said unto Him: Art thou a King, then? Jesus answered: Thou sayest that I am a King. To this end was I born, and for this cause came I into the world, that I should bear witness unto the truth. Everyone that is of the truth heareth My voice. Pilate saith unto Him: What is truth? And when he

*had said this, he went out again unto the Jews and*
*saith unto them: I find in Him no fault at all. But*
*ye have a custom that I should release unto you one*
*at the Passover; will ye therefore that I release unto*
*you the King of the Jews? Then cried they all again,*
*saying: Not this man, but Barabbas. Now Barabbas*
*was a robber.*—JOHN 18:28-40.

LAST week we followed Jesus to the palace of the high
priest, where a preliminary hearing of Jesus was held before Annas, the father-in-law of Caiaphas. John records
this hearing. We know from the accounts of the other
Evangelists that Jesus was condemned by the Sanhedrin
for supposed blasphemy, because He declared under oath
that He was the Son of God.

Tonight's scene presents the trial of Christ before the
Roman governor, Pontius Pilate. The trial before Caiaphas had ended in a sentence of condemnation: "He is
guilty of death." This was the verdict of the court of the
Church, the Sanhedrin. Jesus should die. In other days
that would have ended the matter. The Jews would have
taken Jesus outside the city and stoned Him.

But the Jews at this time were under the jurisdiction of
Rome, and whereas they might conduct their own trials
and even mete out certain punishments up to a certain
number of stripes with the rod, they were not allowed to
carry out any sentence of death. And so they had to take
their case to Pilate, the Roman governor. The spiritual
court had decided that Jesus should die. Now the civil
court should put its stamp of approval on the decision
and carry it out.

John's account reads: "Then led they Jesus from Caiaphas unto the hall of judgment, and it was early" (v. 28a).

It was probably sometime between six and seven o'clock in the morning.

The first characters who pass across the scene in the account are the chief priests and elders and Jews. "They themselves went not into the judgment hall lest they should be defiled, but that they might eat the passover" (v. 28b). The scene before Pilate constantly shifts from the outside to the inside and from the inside to the outside of the judgment hall. It begins outside and then shifts back and forth seven times.

The Jews brought Jesus to the hall of judgment but stayed outside. They would not go inside "lest they become defiled." If they should become defiled, they could not "eat the passover." The passover here spoken of was not the main Passover meal, which had been eaten on Thursday evening. The entire festival which was called the Passover lasted seven days. The phrase "eat the passover" is to be understood as referring to the observation of this whole festival or to the sacrificial meal of this particular day, Friday. They did not want to miss that.

Jesus had accused these same people before of "straining gnats and swallowing camels." Here was a good example in question. Straining gnats by refusing to go into the judgment hall, yet swallowing the camel of committing judicial murder!

"Gnat strainers" and "camel swallowers" are still with us today. We still have those who are sticklers in little things, yet not a bit particular about things much more important. There may be those in church who are more concerned about form and external observances and that everything is liturgically correct than about the more important things which Jesus himself mentioned, as righteousness, justice, truth, consideration, unselfishness, love. Some may be meticulous about smaller obligations to their fellow men and disregard the more important obligations to God.

Next we note our first characters making an accusation by insinuation. Pilate asked: "What accusation do you bring against this Man?" (V. 29.) Jesus was still a prisoner of the Jews, and Pilate would not accept Him before they had made formal charges. They answered: "If He were not an evildoer, we would not have brought Him to you." (V. 30.) They really wanted Pilate to approve their sentence without even conducting a trial. He refused to do so. They accused by insinuation.

So much harm is done merely by insinuation. The devil in the Garden of Eden tempted by insinuation: "Did God really say that you should not eat of the tree? It couldn't possibly be that He meant it." Many a person's character is maligned not by direct accusation, but merely by the innuendos and insinuations of those who seek his harm.

In the third place we see these leaders of the Jews as those who twisted the truth for their own purposes.

They showed this first of all when they came to Pilate with a different accusation from the one for which they had condemned Jesus. They knew that Pilate would not be bothered with a question of their religion, whether or not Jesus had been guilty of blasphemy. So they pretended that they had found Him guilty in their own court of a crime against the Roman government, namely, of perverting the people, forbidding to pay taxes to Caesar, and pretending to be a King. John does not report this but

takes for granted his readers have read about it in St.
Luke's account.

They also showed this tendency to pervert truth for
their own purposes by something which really belongs
into next week's section, namely, by pretending that they
were friends of Caesar and concerned about someone who
might rebel against him, when they knew very well that
they hated everything Roman.

Twisting the truth to suit one's own purposes is a
dangerous thing since it so easily becomes a habit. Truth
or honesty, whether in word or deed, must never be compromised. It is so easy to make oneself believe that twisting the truth is justified under certain circumstances, but
the Scriptures say: "Wherefore putting away lying, speak
every man truth with his neighbor" (Eph. 4:25).

Pilate is the next character to engage our attention in
this scene. In Pilate we see conscience at work, conscience
startled, conscience struggling, conscience compromising,
and, finally, conscience drugged and silenced.

Pilate's conscience was startled in the very presence of
Jesus. He may have heard something about Him, and even
though he had not, the contact with Him here at the trial
was enough to startle him. Pilate had seen many prisoners,
but this one was different. He might have expected Jesus
to want to be set free, but the Prisoner had no such desire
to escape. He might have expected Jesus to make all sorts
of answers in His defense and try to prove Himself innocent; but He did not.

When Pilate finally accepted the case of Jesus on the
basis of the three charges made, he took Him inside to
question Him on those charges beginning with the most
important one: "He says He is Christ, a King." Pilate

probably expected this helpless man to deny the charge, but he was no doubt startled when Jesus answered his question: "Thou sayest that I am a King" (v. 37), in other words: "What you say is true, I am a King." Pilate, face to face with a new situation, was startled.

Next, we see Pilate with a new decision to be made, as a man with a struggling conscience. One of the accounts says that he knew the Jews had given Him over because of envy. He clearly saw his duty. Again and again he declared Him to be innocent. He knew He should be set free, but he feared that he would incur the displeasure of the Jews. Here, then, is his conscience struggling between obedience and expedience.

We see this struggle in the choice he gave them between Jesus and Barabbas. The people began to ask him to do as he usually did at this time of the year, to set a prisoner free. He thought by a master stroke of cleverness to get out of his dilemma; so he offered about the most unacceptable candidate in competition with Jesus. But they chose the unacceptable candidate, Barabbas, of whom John says: "Now Barabbas was a robber" (v. 40).

"What, then, shall I do with Jesus?" he asked the crowd when they demanded Barabbas. "Let Him be crucified!" came the answer. Again we hear Pilate's struggling conscience: "Why, what evil hath He done?"

The struggling conscience began to weaken and next became the compromising conscience. Here is the record. "Then Pilate took Jesus and scourged Him. And the soldiers platted a crown of thorns and put it on His head, and they put on Him a purple robe and said: 'Hail, King of the Jews!' and they smote Him with their hands." (Chap. 19:1-3.) Every time we recite the Apostles' Creed and come to the words "Suffered under Pontius Pilate," we are reminded of Pilate's compromising conscience, for there was no reason why Jesus should have suffered under Pilate. He was merely trying to compromise between what he knew was his duty and what he thought would be best for his selfish interests. He thought by the torture of Christ he could appease His enemies and still remain in their favor.

The drugged and silenced conscience we really find in next week's scene. Suffice it to say now that Pilate, having compromised, was no longer able to stand up and do his duty; conscience lost the battle and went down in defeat.

The application is obvious. God has given to us that little voice which we call conscience. That conscience is molded and shaped in accordance with our training. There is in us by nature a Law by which conscience is governed so that, even though we had never learned a single commandment, we still would have a voice in us which would tell us that it is wrong to kill, to steal, and to commit other gross and obvious sins. However, in addition to being guided by this Natural Law, our conscience is also molded by the religious training we have had. If we have been brought up in a Christian home and have learned the basic, moral laws of God, this voice of conscience will tell us to do what is right and to refuse to do wrong. Pilate's conscience had been trained in the basic principles of Roman justice. He knew what he ought to do. His conscience was telling him to do it, but he disregarded its prompting.

If we have received a Christian training and our conscience is alert, it will often be startled when we come face to face with a situation we have not met before, some temptation which we have never experienced before. Then it begins to prompt us to make a decision. It will tell us to do what we believe to be right.

A struggle may develop. Our conscience tells us to do what we believe to be right, but there are other considerations, expediency, convenience, personal gain, personal pleasure, pleasurable sensation, etc. These may be determining factors. This struggle may go on for some time depending upon how pronounced the issues are. Finally either conscience or the other factors win out.

The result may be an attempt at compromise. We may not go all the way at first. The final result, however, unless there is determined decision to follow strictly the dictates of conscience, will be a drugged and silenced conscience, and the voice that once spoke within us so loudly fades into a whisper and finally is no longer heard. The sin which it kept us from committing becomes a habit and perhaps our master.

What are we doing with our conscience? Is it trained and directed by the Word of God? If so, then heed its voice, even though a thousand powerful influences may be pulling in the other direction.

We now turn to the picture of the judgment seat of Pilate, outside his great hall. We note these characters who play in tonight's story. The chief priests and elders, gnat strainers and camel swallowers, accusing Christ of things of which He was not guilty, twisting truth and making insinuations, calling for His crucifixion. Then we note Pilate, the man whose conscience fought a loosing battle. In the center of the picture is Christ, the King of Truth, who suffered also for the sins we commit against our conscience, who took away all sin by His suffering

and death on the Cross, and who offers us His victory over
sin if we but accept Him as our Savior and Lord.

> Thou hast suffered men to bruise Thee
> That from pain I might be free;
> Falsely did Thy foes accuse Thee,
> Thence I gain security;
> Comfortless Thy soul did languish
> Me to comfort in my anguish.
> Thousand, thousand thanks shall be,
> Dearest Jesus, unto Thee. Amen.

# Behold the Man

Then Pilate therefore took Jesus and scourged Him. And the soldiers platted a crown of thorns and put it on His head, and they put on Him a purple robe and said: Hail, King of the Jews! And they smote Him with their hands. Pilate therefore went forth again and saith unto them: Behold, I bring Him forth to you, that ye may know that I find no fault in Him. Then came Jesus forth wearing the crown of thorns and the purple robe. And Pilate saith unto them: Behold the Man! When the chief priests therefore and officers saw Him, they cried out, saying: Crucify Him, crucify Him! Pilate saith unto them: Take ye Him, and crucify Him; for I find no fault in Him. The Jews answered him: We have a law, and by our law He ought to die, because He made Himself the Son of God.

When Pilate therefore heard that saying, he was the more afraid and went again into the judgment hall and saith unto Jesus: Whence art Thou? But Jesus gave him no answer. Then saith Pilate unto Him: Speakest Thou not unto me? Knowest Thou not that I have power to crucify Thee and have power to release Thee? Jesus answered: Thou couldest have no power at all against Me except it were given thee from above; therefore he that delivered Me unto thee hath the greater sin.

And from thenceforth Pilate sought to release Him; but the Jews cried out, saying: If thou let this Man go,

*thou art not Caesar's friend; whosoever maketh him-
self a king speaketh against Caesar. When Pilate
therefore heard that saying, he brought Jesus forth
and sat down in the judgment seat in a place that is
called the Pavement, but in the Hebrew, Gabbatha.
And it was the preparation of the Passover and about
the sixth hour; and he saith unto the Jews: Behold
your King! But they cried out: Away with Him,
away with Him! Crucify Him! Pilate saith unto
them: Shall I crucify your King? The chief priests
answered: We have no king but Caesar. Then delivered he Him therefore unto them to be crucified.
—JOHN 19:1-16a.*

THE scene this evening keeps us at the judgment seat of
Pilate. The scene changes seven times from the outside
to the inside and from the inside to the outside. It is a
prolonged procedure. The reason was this. Pilate knew
that Christ was innocent. He pronounced Him innocent
again and again; he was seeking some way out, trying to
find some way to release Him. His one plan had failed
according to last week's account when he gave the Jews
the choice between Jesus and Barabbas, the robber, and
they chose Barabbas.

Let us note the characters who pass across the stage in
tonight's scene. First we see Pilate pursuing his policy of
appeasement.

He is Pilate the compromiser. Contrary to all sense of
justice, Pilate gave Jesus over to the soldiers for scourging and mocking. The scourging was a most brutal punishment. It is generally admitted that in the case of Jesus
it was physically so exhausting that it contributed to the
early death of Christ on the Cross. Pilate was surprised
when upon inquiry he found Him already dead at an

early hour. This torture was surely one of the reasons for Christ's breaking down under the load of the Cross.

Pilate permitted also another kind of torture. The soldiers platted a crown of thorns, put it upon Christ's head, and subjected him to ridicule and mockery. "Hail, King of the Jews," they said and struck Him with their hands. (Vv. 2-3.) This was all done with Pilate's permission. The account reads: "Pilate took Jesus and scourged Him" (v. 1). He was responsible. He did it in an effort to appease the mob, hoping that they would be satisfied with something less than crucifixion. He compromised justice.

In the second place we see Pilate as a man ruled by fear. First of all there was the fear of his own Prisoner. Christ had made such an impression upon him that Pilate was afraid.

You will recall that the specific charges which the Jews had brought against Christ were that He was guilty of sedition, guilty of forbidding to pay taxes, and guilty of claiming to be a King. Pilate had investigated these charges and had come back with this conclusion: "I find no indictment in this case." When they cried: "Crucify Him!" Pilate said: "Very well, take ye Him and crucify Him." But they had no authority to put a man to death. "On my part, I find no fault in Him," said Pilate. (V. 6.) The Jews now brought out the real cause for which they wanted His death. In effect they said: "You on your part may not be able to find any indictment, but we on our part have a law by which He ought to die because He made Himself the Son of God." (V. 7.)

"When Pilate heard that saying, he was the more afraid" (v. 8). Jesus the Son of God! Christ had said previously: "My kingdom is not of this world" (Chap. 18:36). So he went inside again for a private questioning with Him and asked Him: "Whence art Thou, where do You come from?" But Jesus would not answer him. (V. 9.) The reason for His silence at this particular time was probably that He had already answered that question.

Another thing which contributed to Pilate's fear was something which John does not record but which is recorded by one of the other Evangelists. His wife sent to him and said: "Have thou nothing to do with that just Man, for I have suffered many things this day in a dream because of Him" (Matt. 27:19). That added to his fear.

The final contribution to his fear was the fear of losing his position and possibly even his life. He was afraid of losing Caesar's friendship. "If thou let this man go," the Jews had said, "thou art not the friend of Caesar" (v. 12). That finally decided the matter for Pilate. We read: "When Pilate therefore heard that saying, he brought Jesus forth and sat down in the judgment seat" (v. 13). He was now ready to pronounce final sentence, that of crucifixion. His mind was made up.

Fear is a very strong impulse which plays into our judgment and our actions more often than we realize. The conquest of fear is considered one of the greatest conquests a man can make. If we were to analyze our attitudes, we would find much of which we are afraid. We might not recognize such fear on the surface, but often it is the underlying cause of many of our actions. Such fear robs us, as it did Pilate, of our happiness and peace of mind. It robs us of our ability to do what should be done, robs us of our best.

We, like Pilate, are often afraid of that which we do

not understand. We are sometimes afraid because of silly superstitions. We are afraid of consequences even though we know that we are right. We may be afraid of losing our position. We are afraid of losing someone's friendship.

The solution for Pilate's fears would have been found in recognizing and accepting the Christ before Him. Pilate had no faith or trust in God. No wonder fear seized him.

It is when we fail in our trust in God that we fear. We cannot trust and fear at the same time. We may oscillate between the two, we may be afraid one moment and trust the next, but when complete trust takes possession of us, fear vanishes. The Psalmist says: "The Lord is my Light and my Salvation; whom shall I fear? The Lord is the Strength of my life; of whom shall I be afraid?" (Ps. 27:1.) Jesus says: "Let not your heart be troubled, neither let it be afraid" (John 14:27). The fearful heart is the heart which does not recognize fully and accept completely the Christ. Let Christ take hold, let Christ in, let Him fill your life and your heart, and fear will disappear. "What time I am afraid, I will trust in Thee" (Ps. 56:3).

Looking at Pilate from another angle, we see him at one moment the judge and the next moment the judged. With all the arrogance of a Roman judge he upbraided Jesus for not answering: "Speakest Thou not unto me? Knowest Thou not that I have power to crucify Thee and have power to release Thee?" (V. 10.) But Jesus answered: "Thou couldest have no power at all against Me except it were given thee from above." We suddenly notice the judge being judged by Jesus, the very Judge of the earth. He continues: "Therefore he that delivered Me unto thee hath the greater sin." (V. 11.)

The Prisoner dares to say in effect to the judge: "You are guilty. You are not as guilty as Caiaphas and the Jews who delivered Me to you, but you are guilty." Pilate had to say of Jesus: "He is not guilty"; but when Jesus becomes the Judge, he cannot say the same thing for Pilate. His verdict is: "You are guilty!"

Jesus here indicates that there is such a thing as degree of guilt. Not everyone has the same proportion of guilt. Caiaphas, whose knowledge of Jesus should have been more complete, is more guilty than Pilate, who may not have had the same opportunity. This truth is taught elsewhere in Scripture, in Luke 12:47-48: "Unto whomsoever much is given, of him shall be much required; and to whom men have committed much, of him they will ask the more"; and in Matt. 10:15: "It shall be more tolerable for the land of Sodom and Gomorrha in the Day of Judgment than for that city," the city which rejects Christ. You and I are especially privileged. Much will be required of us.

Pilate became a total failure as a judge. He was willing to release Jesus, but finally, because of the pressure of the multitude, because of the fear for his position, he pronounced sentence. "Then delivered he Him unto them to be crucified. And they took Jesus and led Him away." (V. 16.) In reading the story we naturally try to reconstruct it. Perhaps we sympathize just a little with Pilate and in our own imagination try to help him find a way out, but he refused all of the openings. He did make one last feeble effort before he pronounced sentence when he said: "Behold your King" (v. 14). Would they call for their "King's" crucifixion? He had miscalculated before, and he did it again. They demanded His crucifixion, and he yielded. Conscience, Pilate's conscience, had lost its battle.

The other character we note in our scene this evening is Jesus. Here is John's simple description: "Then came Jesus forth, wearing the crown of thorns and the purple robe. And Pilate saith unto them: "Behold the Man" (v. 5). That is the title of several paintings of this scene, "Ecce Homo!" "Behold the man!" Let us do just that, behold the man.

We behold Him as the great Sufferer. He had come from the terrible scourging, still wearing the crown of thorns, still wearing the robe of mockery. That is all that some people see in Him, a man who suffered because of his ideals, a man who suffered because of envy and jealousy of his enemies, a man who suffered for a cause.

Anyone can behold Him in that way. Even the devil can behold Him in that light. Even His enemies beheld that in Him. Pilate saw Him in that manner. As a matter of fact, it was this that Pilate wanted the Jews to behold, and he held out the faint hope that, beholding Him thus, they would be moved to pity and be satisfied. They did behold Him, but their reaction was one of scorn: "Away with Him!"

We behold Jesus as the patient and silent Sufferer. "Who, when He was reviled, reviled not again." "He openeth not his mouth." Some people would see only that in Him and would learn only patience from beholding Him. But there is more than that.

Pilate not only said: "Behold the Man," but significantly said a moment later: "Behold your King" (v. 14). That is the way we must behold the Man, namely, as our King.

He came forth wearing the crown of thorns and the purple robe. John saw in that the real truth that here was the King, crowned, it is true, in mockery and robed in royal purple for ridicule, but nevertheless King. Pilate had asked Him: "Art Thou a King?" and Jesus had accepted the title. He was a King indeed, not in a kingdom of this world, but of another; not in a kingdom that deals only with men's material welfare, but one which includes especially their spiritual concern, a kingdom of souls. This is Jesus, King of Kings and Lord of Lords.

That brings us to the other characters in the scene, namely the people. What did they do when Pilate said: "Behold the Man!"? They only cried out: "Crucify Him! Crucify Him!" (V. 6.) And when Pilate, uttering a truth more real than he ever imagined, said: "Behold your King," they shouted all the more: "Away with Him! Away with Him! Crucify Him! Crucify Him!" (V. 15.)

Jesus is still presented to the people, He still comes forth wearing the crown of thorns and the purple robe. Every Christian service that is conducted, every truly Christian radio broadcast presents Christ to men and says in effect: "Behold Him, Behold the Man! Behold your King!" This Lenten season once more brings Him before us with the injunction "Behold the Man! Behold your King!"

The world still cries with the chief priests and elders: "Away with Him! Away with Him!" not always in audible voices, but in a manner that is more subtle but no less final, "Away with Him!" The multitude is offended at the crown of thorns, the Gospel of a suffering Savior, and says: "Away with Him! Give us another brand of religion, another kind of Christ!" The world has no place for

Him in its program, and so it rejects Him by neglect. The sorry mess in which the world finds itself today is evidence enough that all but a few faithful followers have cried for His crucifixion, for His elimination.

Somewhere in that crowd that day must have been the writer of this Gospel, faithful John, who writes so vividly and yet so tenderly about this scene. When Pilate said: "Behold the Man," he must have thought in his own heart: "Yes, I behold Him, He is my Savior, not only a man, but the Christ, the Son of God." When Pilate said: "Behold your King," in his own heart John must have said: "Yes, He is my King, He is my Lord and Master, my King, to whom I am subject, my King, who rules my life, my all."

We stand with the crowd. Today, yes, tonight, when Jesus in our Gospel appears before us wearing the crown of thorns and the purple robe, let us with surrendering faith behold the Man as our Savior who suffered and died in our stead, who wore the crown of thorns and suffered ridicule and mockery in our place, who went to the Cross to die for our sins. Let us also behold Him as our King and Lord, to whom we yield our lives and in whose service we stand ready to do His bidding.

Now let us turn to the picture entitled "Ecce Homo," or "Behold the Man." We see Pilate pleading with the people: "Look at Him, look what I have permitted to have done to Him, are you not satisfied?" Here is Pilate the judge, yet judged here by the Prisoner—guilty! Here is Pilate the fearful man, afraid of his Prisoner, afraid of the people, afraid of Caesar, a total failure. Here is Christ the Man, as the great and silent and patient Sufferer, yet Christ the King, whose crown of thorns and purple robe, though intended for mockery, were really a symbol of what in reality He was, the King of Kings. Finally, we see the people clamoring for His crucifixion, rejecting the Lord who bought them.

> Grant that I Thy Passion view
> With repentant grieving,
> Nor Thee crucify anew
> By unholy living.
> How could I refuse to shun
> Every sinful pleasure
> Since for me God's only Son
> Suffered without measure? Amen.

# Christ on the Cross

They took Jesus and led Him away. And He, bearing His Cross, went forth into a place called the place of a skull, which is called in the Hebrew Golgotha, where they crucified Him and two other with Him, on either side one, and Jesus in the midst.

And Pilate wrote a title and put it on the Cross. And the writing was: JESUS OF NAZARETH, THE KING OF THE JEWS. This title, then, read many of the Jews; for the place where Jesus was crucified was nigh to the city; and it was written in Hebrew and Greek and Latin. Then said the chief priests of the Jews to Pilate: Write not: The King of the Jews; but that He said: I am King of the Jews. Pilate answered: What I have written I have written.

Then the soldiers, when they had crucified Jesus, took His garments and made four parts, to every soldier a part; and also His coat. Now the coat was without seam, woven from the top throughout. They said therefore among themselves: Let us not rend it, but cast lots for it, whose it shall be—that the Scripture might be fulfilled, which saith: They parted My raiment among them, and for My vesture they did cast lots. These things therefore the soldiers did.

Now there stood by the Cross of Jesus His mother, and His mother's sister, Mary, the wife of Cleophas, and Mary Magdalene. When Jesus therefore saw His mother and the disciple standing by whom He loved, He saith unto His mother: Woman, behold thy son!

*Then saith He to the disciple: Behold thy mother!*
*And from that hour that disciple took her unto his*
*own home.*

*After this, Jesus knowing that all things were now*
*accomplished, that the Scripture might be fulfilled,*
*saith: I thirst. Now there was set a vessel full of*
*vinegar; and they filled a sponge with vinegar and*
*put it upon hyssop and put it to His mouth. When*
*Jesus therefore had received the vinegar, He said: It*
*is finished! And He bowed His head and gave up the*
*ghost.*—JOHN 19:16b-30.

TONIGHT'S scene takes us out to Calvary, the place of
crucifixion, or Golgotha, which means "the place of a
skull."

The first persons introduced to us are included in the
phrase "they crucified Him." John passes over all the horrible details of the crucifixion and merely reports: "They
crucified Him." Our attention centers on the word "they."
Who are those included in the word "they"?

When Peter preached his sermon at Jerusalem on
Pentecost, he said: "Ye men of Israel, Him ye have taken
and by wicked hands have crucified and slain" (Acts
2:22-23). Peter leaves no doubt about it, the Jews to
whom he was speaking crucified Christ. Again and again
we hear it said today: "The Jews did not crucify Christ,
the Romans did it." That is very true, the Bible says: "Ye
by wicked hands" did it. But it is still "ye men of Israel."
In our text it is "they," and when you read the account,
you will see that "they" refers to the chief priests and the
people. The only reason they did not carry out the actual
crucifixion was that they were not allowed by the Roman

law to do so. But the Bible still places the blame for it
on them. "They crucified Him."

It is not nearly so important what they did to Christ
many years ago as what they do to Him today. No Hebrew
is held to account for what his forefathers did by crucifying Jesus if he himself does not reject Him today. God's
Word tells us that God "visits the iniquity of the fathers
upon the children unto the third and fourth generation of
them that hate Him," not upon those who love and accept
Him.

Lest we point the finger of accusation, however, at a
race or people and accuse them solely of the crucifixion
of our Lord, let us turn to other passages of Scripture
which tell us the real cause of Christ's death. Here is John
the Baptist pointing to Jesus, the sinless One, as he says:
"Behold the Lamb of God, which taketh away the sin of
the world" (John 1:29). There is the real explanation. So
we sing in one of our hymns, "Ah! I also and my sin
Wrought Thy deep affliction; this indeed the cause hath
been Of Thy crucifixion."

When we then read: "They crucified Him," the accusing finger points also at you and at me. Our sins of blasphemy, jealousy, dishonesty, spiritual arrogance, self-
righteousness, gossip, slander, deceit, covetousness, these
drove the nails. The Romans and the Jews were merely
the agents through whom we by our sins brought about
Christ's death. Those included in the word "they" are
the Jews who were responsible for the crucifixion, the
Roman soldiers who carried it out, and all mankind, for
whose sins the crucifixion took place.

The next character who appears this evening is a character off stage. He is Pilate. We read that Pilate wrote a

superscription. (V. 19.) "And the title was written in Hebrew and Greek and Latin," in the national language, so the Jews could read it, in the official language of the government, and in the language of the common people of that day. (V. 20.) Incidentally, the fact that this title was written in these languages accounts for the fact that there are several different versions, Matthew: "This is Jesus, the King of the Jews," Mark: "The King of the Jews," Luke: "This is the King of the Jews," and John: "Jesus of Nazareth, the King of the Jews" (v. 19). Everyone of them included the thought "King of the Jews." Those who point to these passages to show that there are discrepancies in the Bible forget that the title might have been worded in a different fashion in each one of the languages.

The Jews objected to the title. They came to Pilate and asked him to change it. They wanted him to change it to "He said: 'I am the King of the Jews.'" (v. 21). They hated the superscription, and Pilate knew it. He had written what he knew would annoy them. They had annoyed him no end. Here was a chance to get even with them.

Pilate insisted: "What I have written, I have written" (v. 22). We rather admire him for his stand. But he should have taken a firm stand sooner. It looks very much like an attempt to save his face.

So the superscription remained that day on the Cross and remains true to the present day. Jesus was the King of the Jews and the King of all mankind.

We find that superscription on the crucifixes that adorn our altars and are worn by Christians. Above the head of Jesus there are usually four letters, INRI. The I in Latin is our English J, and so these four letters stand for these four Latin words: "Jesus Nazarenus Rex Judaeorum," which, translated, means, "Jesus, the Nazarene, the King of the Jews."

The rest of the story brings us to the foot of the Cross, where we find two groups of people, the soldiers and the friends of Jesus. The soldiers first of all engage the attention of John. Their gruesome work was finished. The four soldiers in charge could now go about other things. The first was to divide the spoils. (Vv. 23-24.) The clothing of the victim belonged to the executioners. Apparently there were four pieces of clothing besides the main tunic which Jesus wore. Some have conjectured that these were the outer robe, the shoes, or sandals, the belt, and the headgear. Because these were of unequal value, it was necessary to cast lots between them whose they should be. The tunic or main garment was of one piece, useless if divided, so, rather than divide it, they cast lots also for that piece, whose it should be. It is this garment which has been made the subject of the book *The Robe,* by Lloyd Douglas, a best seller of sometime ago.

Notice the soldiers casting lots for the clothes of Jesus, untouched by the tragedy which was being enacted before their eyes. One of them did change his mind in the course of that day. He confessed: "Truly this was a righteous man and the Son of God." Here at the beginning, all of them were altogether unmoved by what was going on before them.

The reason for their attitude is obvious. They were used to it. They had become calloused. There is always a danger for us in this respect. It is so easy to become calloused. Something that would at one time shock us ceases to affect us when we experience it often enough or read of it or hear of it often enough. It is a dangerous thing to become "unshockable." The tragedies and horrifying events which are being enacted before us in the world and which are reported in the daily papers today will have a callousing effect upon us if we do not constantly and consciously sensitize ourselves to them. We must remain sensitive to the misfortunes of others, compassionate and sympathetic. We must remain incapable of "gambling below a cross."

The compassion we find altogether lacking in the hardened soldiers we find present in the Victim on the Cross. The opportunity for its expression was occasioned by another group of people standing at the Cross, generally accepted as five in number, one man and four women, Mary, the mother of Jesus, Salome, her sister, Mary, the wife of Cleophas, Mary Magdalene, and John. The man was, according to John's account, "the disciple whom Jesus loved," therefore John himself. (V. 25.) In the midst of His agony, as the "pains of hell gradually got hold of Him," Jesus permitted His eyes to fall upon this group, His own mother and the others. A sword was piercing her soul as Simeon had once prophesied when he held Jesus in his arms as an infant. Jesus knew it, and so He said to her: "Woman, behold thy son!"; and as His eyes passed over to John, He said to him: "Behold thy mother!" (Vv. 25-26.) In the midst of His agonies for the redemption of the world Jesus thought of His mother.

We sometimes excuse ourselves for lack of consideration and concern for others on the ground that we are so busy, occupied with so many things that we just forget, forget sometimes the common courtesies and thoughtfulness that make life so much more pleasant for those with whom we come in contact. Jesus here in the midst of the greatest project for mankind is not too busy or too occupied to think of someone else.

Incidentally, we notice that Jesus provides for Mary and does not lay upon her any obligation for providing for others. We mention this because, in the maze of the superstitious Mariolatry of the Roman Church, Mary has been made the great "caretaker" of the faithful. Nowhere does Jesus ever indicate this role for her. He provided for her care.

There were other things that took place during the six hours that Christ was hanging upon the Cross from 9 o'clock in the forenoon to 3 o'clock in the afternoon, but John passes them over because they are recorded by the other Evangelists. We think of the assuring word of Jesus to the malefactor who turned to Him in repentance: "Verily I say unto thee, today shalt thou be with Me in Paradise." We think of the darkness that covered the earth from noon to three o'clock. We think of the agonizing cry from the depths of Christ's suffering: "My God, My God, why hast Thou forsaken Me?" These things had all taken place, and now John records significantly: "Jesus knowing that all things were now accomplished, that the Scripture might be fulfilled, saith: 'I thirst'" (v. 28). This is the first word that passed His lips to indicate physical suffering. He did not say these words until He knew that everything was accomplished. The soldiers, who stood by, gave Him something to drink, called vinegar in our text, perhaps sour wine.

Thereupon followed the sixth word from the Cross, for "when Jesus had received the vinegar, He said: 'It is finished!' " (v. 30a). The work which He had been given to do was completed. This was His cry of victory.

"And He bowed His head and gave up the ghost" (v. 30b). Everyone of the accounts states it that way. They all say: "He yielded up the spirit." It was a voluntary act on His part. We have called attention to the fact that this is evident all the way through His Passion. When He was taken captive in the Garden of Gethsemane, He said: "Rise, let us be going," Let us be going out to meet My captors. He went forth to them. He reminded Pilate that he had no power over Him, but that His power was given Him from above. We read of Him at the beginning of to-night's account: "He went forth bearing His Cross" (v. 17), not "they took Him out," but "He went forth." So here also: "He gave up the ghost." It was a voluntary act. We are taken back to the time when, with all of His enemies around Him, He said: "No man taketh My life from Me, but I lay it down of Myself. I have power to lay it down, and I have power to take it again" (John 10:18). And as we see Him here laying it down, we know it was for us He died, giving His life in place of ours. The Cross has been given all kinds of meanings, it has been declared a symbol of so many things, but this one thing it means to the born-again Christian: Christ here gave Himself for me, He died for me. The Cross is for me the symbol of my salvation.

As we now turn to the picture, we see those whom the text means by "they," namely those guilty of the crucifixion of Christ, symbolizing all of us who by our sins put Christ there. We see the soldiers "gambling below the cross," calloused to the tragedy being enacted before them.

We see Christ caring for His mother, and we see Christ giving Himself for us.

> When I survey the wondrous Cross
>   On which the Prince of Glory died,
> My richest gain I count but loss
>   And pour contempt on all my pride.
>
> Were the whole realm of nature mine,
>   That were a tribute far too small;
> Love so amazing, so divine,
>   Demands my soul, my life, my all. Amen.

# The Burial of Christ

The Jews, therefore, because it was the preparation, that the bodies should not remain upon the cross on the Sabbath day (for that Sabbath day was an high day), besought Pilate that their legs might be broken and that they might be taken away. Then came the soldiers and brake the legs of the first and of the other which was crucified with Him. But when they came to Jesus and saw that He was dead already, they brake not His legs; but one of the soldiers with a spear pierced His side, and forthwith came there out blood and water. And he that saw it bare record, and his record is true; and he knoweth that he saith true, that ye might believe. For these things were done, that the Scripture should be fulfilled: A bone of Him shall not be broken. And again another Scripture saith: They shall look on Him whom they pierced.

And after this, Joseph of Arimathaea, being a disciple of Jesus, but secretly for fear of the Jews, besought Pilate that he might take away the body of Jesus; and Pilate gave him leave. He came therefore and took the body of Jesus. And there came also Nicodemus, which at the first came to Jesus by night, and brought a mixture of myrrh and aloes, about an hundred pound weight. Then took they the body of Jesus and wound it in linen clothes with the spices, as the manner of the Jews is to bury. Now in the place where He was crucified there was a garden, and in the garden a new sepulchre, wherein was never man *yet laid. There laid they Jesus therefore because of the Jews' preparation day; for the sepulchre was nigh at hand.*—JOHN 19:31-42.

THIS evening we come to the last scene in the story we have followed since Ash Wednesday. In the words of the well-known hymn we have "gone to dark Gethsemane," we have "followed to the judgment hall," we have "climbed Calvary's mournful mountain," there to hear Him cry: "It is finished!" and tonight we go to the tomb "where they laid His breathless clay."

As we have allowed these scenes to unfold before us, we have considered the characters that have passed across the stage—Judas, who betrayed Him, the soldiers who captured Him, the chief priest who condemned Him, the disciple, Peter, who denied Him, Pilate, who judged Him, the people who rejected Him, the soldiers who crucified Him, the people who watched them, and the Savior, who gave Himself into death. This evening, as we consider His burial, we observe those who in death were nearest to Him. Of this time it has been said: "The ugliest and darkest days in human history were the days when Jesus was dead." Think for a moment what it would be like if this were the end of the story tonight! "Jesus is dead!" We are all conscious, however, that something else is still to be said, and above the awful words of tonight's lesson "There laid they Jesus" we cannot help but hear the angel's message about that same place: "He is not here, He is risen."

The first verses of this section (31-37) tell us of the body of Jesus in the hands of His enemies, the last verses (38-42) tell us of the body of Jesus in the hands of His friends.

First we find the Jews requesting the removal of the bodies from the crosses. "The Jews therefore, because it was the preparation, that the bodies should not remain upon the cross on the Sabbath day, for that Sabbath day was a high day"—it was the Sabbath of the Passover season—"besought Pilate that their legs might be broken and that they might be taken away" (v. 31). Their request is made on the ground of religion. The Romans simply permitted the bodies to decay on the cross, but the Jews took them down the same day in accordance with their law: "And if a man have committed a sin worthy of death and he be to be put to death and thou hang him on a tree, his body shall not remain all night upon the tree, but thou shalt in any wise bury him that day (for he that is hanged is accursed of God); that thy land be not defiled, which the Lord, thy God, giveth thee for an inheritance" (Deut. 21:22). So they were strictly within the limits of their law when they asked Pilate to have the bodies taken down; but we see them here in the same light that we saw them when they refused to go into the judgment hall ("lest they should be defiled," chap. 18:28), "straining gnats and swallowing camels," insisting upon the ritual of religion while violating the very essence of it.

We hear of Pilate here again in an off-stage position, for while John tells nothing about it because it was recorded elsewhere, we do read in another Gospel that Pilate sent for the centurion to inquire whether Jesus were already dead. Could it be that his fears were haunting him again?

Pilate allowed the Jews to have their way, and the soldiers went, by Pilate's order, to break the legs and take the body down. This breaking of the legs was a cruel hastening of death. Some have conjectured that another

reason for using this particular procedure was that sometimes the bodies were removed before the criminals were
dead, and this assured no chance for escape.

Significantly we read: "Then came the soldiers and
brake the legs of the first and of the other. . . . But when
they came to Jesus and saw that he was dead already, they
brake not His legs." (Vv. 32-33.) Why did they wait
with Jesus till the last? Perhaps the centurion in charge,
who had been so deeply impressed by Jesus, wanted it that
way. Since Jesus was dead already, there was no need
to break His legs.

One of the soldiers pierced the Savior's side, and immediately there came out blood and water. John adds that
he saw this all, and he is telling it all "that ye might
believe." (Vv. 34-35.) Much has been made of the fact
that blood and water flowed out of Jesus' side. Some med-
ical authorities tell us that this could not have been the
case, and so some have contended that John wants to
record a miracle. It almost seems so since he adds immediately, "that ye might believe," reminding us of the key
verse to the whole book of John: "These (signs) are written that ye might believe" (chap. 20:31).

John is emphasizing just one thing: Jesus was dead.
He is indicating that there is no doubt about it, Jesus was
so certainly dead that the soldiers did not bother to break
his legs, dead because of the fatal wound inflicted by the
spear, or lance, thrust in His side. It excludes all possibilities of a so-called "death sleep," or swoon. John wants
to record the fact that Jesus was dead, so that he can
establish also the fact that Jesus arose from death. Here
he indicates: "I saw it with my own eyes, Jesus was dead."

There are those who have found a symbolism in the

blood and water that flowed from the side of our Savior. As water has cleansing power, so, and much more so, the blood of Jesus Christ, God's Son, cleanses us from all sin. This reference has been used in the hymn "Rock of Ages":

> Let the water and the blood,
> From Thy riven side which flowed,
> Be of sin the double cure,
> Cleanse me from its guilt and power.

John calls attention to the fact that there was a twofold fulfillment of prophecy. In Exodus the Jews were told that the Passover lamb should be a perfect lamb, not a bone should be broken either before or during its preparation and eating. So Jesus, the perfect Passover Lamb of God, should likewise not suffer His bones to be broken. (V. 36.) The other prophecy was that of Zechariah, which said: "They shall look on Him whom they pierced" (v. 37). The soldiers and those about the Cross looked on Him whom they pierced. So we look on Him whom they pierced, and as we look in faith, we are saved by the blood that He shed.

Now we see the body of Jesus taken over by the hands of His friends. His body was taken down from the Cross. A new man now appears on the scene. His name is Joseph of Arimathaea.

We are told where he came from, Arimathaea.

Matthew tells us that he was rich. This is also evident from the fact that he owned a grave, a new one, in a garden, hewn out of the rock, not far away. Mark tells us he was honorable and that he waited for the Kingdom of God. Luke tells us that he was a member of the Sanhedrin, the Jewish court which condemned Jesus, but that he "had not consented to the counsel and deed of them." He had not voted for Christ's death. John tells us he was a disciple, a believer in Christ; however, a secret disciple. That was nothing unusual. He was a member of the group which had threatened expulsion to anyone who dared to claim to be a disciple of Christ. He was a disciple of Jesus, but "secretly for fear of the Jews" (v. 38). How many times are we not disciples, but "secretly for fear of somebody." It is easy to confess being a disciple here in God's house. It is easy to confess our loyalty to and fellowship with Christ in our hymns, to sing: "Jesus, Thou art mine forever," when everybody else around us is singing it; but when we stand alone, when we run the danger of being ridiculed, that is often another matter.

Certainly being a secret disciple is better than being no disciple at all. We cannot but wonder, however, what the influence of such a man as Joseph might have been if he had been a bold and confessing disciple of Christ. The strange thing about it is that, when it apparently was most difficult to be bold about his discipleship, he showed that boldness. When Christ had been crucified and there was the danger that his followers might be next on the list, Joseph of Arimathaea identifies himself with Jesus by requesting the body of Christ. He cast his fears aside and, according to Mark's account, dared to go to Pilate so that he might provide a decent burial for Christ in his own new grave, thereby fulfilling the Scripture which says: "He made His grave with the rich in His death" (Is. 53:9).

The next character introduced in our account is Nicodemus. "And there came also Nicodemus, which at the first came to Jesus by night, and brought a mixture of myrrh and aloes, about an hundred pound weight" (v. 39).

John tells us that he was the man who at the beginning of John's ministry came to Him. We recall how Nicodemus came to Jesus under the cover of darkness and how Jesus instructed him unto his salvation. He came by night because he was afraid, but he came. John tells us elsewhere that Nicodemus, too, was a member of the Sanhedrin. He apparently also had not voted for Christ's death. Now made bold by the death of Christ, Nicodemus comes to assist in the burial. He reveals himself as a true follower. A crisis often reveals the true follower and the false. The crises of our lives are testing grounds. How do we measure up under test?

Nicodemus and Joseph of Arimathaea must have made arrangements to meet at Golgotha. We draw this conclusion from the fact that Joseph arranged for the linen cloths, and Nicodemus brought along the spices, about a hundred pounds, "as was the custom of the Jews to bury." "They therefore took the body of Jesus and bound it with linen bands together with the spices." (V. 40.)

When Peter, the boastful disciple, and the others had fled and were nowhere to be found, it was Nicodemus and Joseph, two fearful disciples, who became courageous and buried the body of Jesus.

Joseph offers his own grave. "In the place where He was crucified there was a garden" (v. 41). Here we have the Cross and the garden. In a garden man lost life. In a garden life should be restored to man. In a garden we plant the seeds that spring up to life. In a garden we plant the bodies that spring up to everlasting life. In a garden the body of Christ was planted to come forth to life.

Besides those whom John indicates as present, Matthew

also mentions women. We cannot help but believe that John, the writer of our Gospel, must have been there. Loving hands all, willing to offer their last services to one whom they loved! We commend them for their loving service. They thought they were rendering their service for a dead Christ. How much more should we be willing to offer services unto a living Christ! Those who loved Him treated Him as dead. John tells us in the next chapter: "As yet they knew not the Scripture that He must rise again from the dead" (chap. 20:9). They still loved Him even in death, and they still apparently believed in Him. Faith was still there, but it was being sorely tested. In the words of the disciples on the way to Emmaus, they trusted that it had been He who should have redeemed Israel. But His enemies had apparently triumphed. He was dead.

His enemies thought that they had won, and they were glad. His friends thought that He was defeated, and they were sad. But God was preparing for the day that would be as bright with joy as this one was dark with grief, when by the angel message the news could be declared, the news of the defeat of sin and evil, the news of the victory over death: "He lives!"

We cannot follow Christ to the grave without being extremely thankful to God for all that He has done for us through His Son, that His love prompted Him to send Jesus into death for us, that through Him He forgives us all our sins and opens heaven's door to us, that He washes our robes and makes them white in the blood of the Lamb and that He raised Christ from the grave so that we are able to say as we lay to rest loved ones who have fallen asleep in Jesus: "O Death, where is thy sting?

O Grave, where is thy victory? . . . But thanks be to God, which giveth us the victory through our Lord Jesus Christ!" (1 Cor. 15:55, 57.)

Viewing the picture, we see the dead Christ with the spear wound in His side; the crown of thorns has been laid aside; two men, Joseph and Nicodemus, in the right center background, secret and fearful disciples now become bold; the centurion, who according to the artist followed to the grave; John, the disciple, standing toward the left; other friends who lovingly laid Him to rest; all of them here sowing in tears, not knowing that the time should soon come when they would reap in joy, not knowing that "weeping may endure for the night, but joy cometh in the morning." We ought to recall this scene when we re-enact it under our own personal conditions, knowing that we, as these friends of Christ, shall know the joy of resurrection.

> Asleep in Jesus! Blessed sleep,
>     From which none ever wakes to weep;
> A calm and undisturbed repose,
>     Unbroken by the last of foes.
>
> Asleep in Jesus! Oh, for me
>     May such a blissful refuge be!
> Securely shall my ashes lie
>     And wait the summons from on high. Amen.

# Good Friday Signs and Wonders

*Many other signs truly did Jesus in the presence of His disciples, which are not written in this book; but these are written, that ye might believe that Jesus is the Christ, the Son of God, and that, believing, ye might have life through His name.*—John 20:30-31. Cf. Matt. 27:45-60; Mark 15:33-47.

Good Friday and Golgotha are full of signs and wonders. In the words of a well-known hymn we sing: "Wonder of wonders, oh, how can it be? Jesus the Crucified pleads for me." It is a wonder, something marvelous, that Jesus prays: "Father, forgive them, for they know not what they do." These words and others which He spoke, and what took place during the hours that He was hanging upon the Cross, will ever be a cause of wonder.

It is a great wonder that the Cross itself has become the symbol of victory. It was not intended as such by those who made it. Intended to stand as the emblem of defeat, Christ completely reversed its purpose! He made it the sign of victory!

Christ's whole life was full of miracles, signs, and wonders. He was born into the world in a miraculous way of the Virgin Mary. When He went about His work, He performed signs and wonders that people might believe that He was sent from God. The lame walked at His touch, the deaf heard at His command, the blind saw when He opened their eyes.

St. John records some of these signs and wonders, but he adds: "Many other signs truly did Jesus . . . which are not written in this book" (v. 30). This is true especially of the signs and wonders of Good Friday. Most of these we learn from the other Evangelists. The great purpose of the signs and wonders which Jesus performed during His life as well as those which took place at His death is given in the words of our text: "That ye might believe" (v. 31).

Let us look at a few of these miracles of Good Friday.

The first we note was the miraculous darkness which spread over the land from the sixth to the ninth hour, from noon to 3 o'clock in the afternoon. This was not a mere eclipse of the sun, since we know the Passover occurred at the time of full moon, and an eclipse of the sun is impossible at that time of the month. The world hid its eye, as it were, from the horrible scene that was being enacted on Calvary's hill as Christ, God's Son, died for the sins of men.

> Well might the sun in darkness hide
> And shut his glories in
> When God, the mighty Maker, died
> For man the creature's sin.

Another miracle of that Good Friday which engages our attention was the earthquake. We read: "The earth did quake, and the rocks rent." Call it coincidence, if you will, that these things took place exactly at the time of Jesus' death. Some of the greatest miracles of God have seemed like coincidences. Some of us here can point to prayers answered in a miraculous fashion, and yet their answers appeared very much like coincidences.

Whether we call the phenomena of Good Friday miracles or coincidences, the Bible links them with Christ's death on the Cross. The forces of nature were disturbed, as it were, when the very Creator gave Himself into that shameful death on the Cross.

One of the most significant miracles which took place at the time of Christ's death was the rending of the veil in the Temple. The account very definitely links this rending with the very moment of Christ's death. "He yielded up His Spirit, and the veil in the Temple was rent." This was not merely a result of the earthquake, for the Temple itself was apparently unharmed. This was a supernatural phenomenon, intended to teach this very definite truth that, when Christ gave Himself up for the sins of mankind, the wall or partition between God and man was broken down. The veil in the Temple was a heavy partition curtain of the thickness of a man's hand, separating the Holy Place from the Holy of Holies, symbolizing that there was something which separates man from the presence of God. Once each year, on the Great Day of Atonement, the high priest offered a double sacrifice for his own and for the people's sins and then, taking some of the blood from the innocent victim of the sacrifice, went into the Holy of Holies to sprinkle this blood upon the mercy seat of the Ark of the Covenant for the atonement of his own and of the people's sins. This whole ceremony, of course, had merely prefigured the atonement through Christ and His entrance into the Holy of Holies of heaven with the blood of the everlasting covenant, His own precious blood. Now that He had accomplished this entrance, the veil was no longer needed. Christ, the Great High Priest, had once and for all entered the Holy of Holies of heaven by His own blood and made atonement for our sins.

So in our churches the altar is not veiled from the congregation. The sanctuary, though considered a sacred place in the church because of its purposes, is entered by the faithful when they approach the Lord's Table. The very priesthood of any select group was done away with when the veil in the Temple was rent. Each Christian is now a member of the "royal priesthood," having direct access to God through Christ.

The rending of the veil in the Temple was probably the most significant of all of the miracles accompanying the death of Jesus on the Cross.

Still another miracle took place. We read: "And the graves were opened, and many bodies of the saints which slept arose and came out of the graves after His resurrection and went into the holy city and appeared unto many." We know no more about it than just this statement of the fact. Christ had by His death conquered death, and here was a miracle in evidence of that fact.

There were still other miracles which took place on Calvary, not only in the inanimate rocks of the fields and the curtain in the Temple, but in people, in the souls of those for whom Christ reached out in pity and love and forgiveness.

The greatest miracle is not a miracle that breaks a rock, but the miracle that melts a heart of stone; not the miracle that brings the physically dead to life, but that which revives the spiritually dead and makes them alive. The conversion of a soul is still the greatest event on earth over which the angels rejoice and with which God Himself is pleased. Jesus spoke of such miracles when He said: "Greater works than these shall he [the believer] do" (John 14:12).

The conversion of a soul is nothing less than a miracle, for by itself it cannot be converted, it cannot become warmed, it cannot come to life. This must be done to it, and God Himself alone is able to bring about the sinner's conversion.

It was a miracle, then, when after he heard Christ pray for His enemies and observed His whole attitude on the Cross, the one malefactor turned from a blasphemer to a believer. He started out by railing on Christ together with the other thief, but later on he requested: "Lord, remember me when Thou comest into Thy Kingdom." A self-confessed criminal, acknowledging that he was getting what was coming to Him, pleads for forgiveness, pleads for mercy, for heaven. Here is a miracle greater than any earthquake.

Still another miracle took place when the centurion, going about his heartless work in routine fashion, calloused to this sort of thing because it was his every day's business, began to notice something different about this crucifixion from the others in which he had taken part. When he noticed how Jesus did not gradually expire, but with a loud voice gave up the spirit, noticed His patience, heard the prayer which Jesus prayed also for him, noticed all of the phenomenal circumstances surrounding this Man's death, he exclaimed: "Certainly this was a righteous Man and the Son of God." Another miracle of grace had taken place.

Still another miracle took place in the two men Joseph of

Arimathaea and Nicodemus, both men in high positions, who had been afraid to own their discipleship with Christ, but who now came and asked for the body of Jesus that they might bury it. When their fears were changed to courage and their hesitancy into willing service, a miracle took place on that Good Friday.

The greatest miracle, of course, is the fact of the Cross itself, that here on a Cross God's Son died for the sins of men. The miracle of God's love can never be explained nor fully comprehended, but here we see its evidence. Christ died that we might live.

Not only was that a miracle when Christ died for us on the Cross, but it becomes a miracle of grace when God by His Holy Spirit leads us to accept that truth so that it becomes real and meaningful for us individually. The acceptance of this truth changes the individual from death to life. You and I were born anew when by faith we accepted the fact and implications of Good Friday, when by faith we embraced the Cross as the evidence of God's grace toward us. To us individually this is the greatest wonder of Good Friday, that we believe. This, according to our text, is the purpose of all signs and wonders in connection with Christ.

Still another miracle will take place before us this very evening, on this Good Friday. We shall celebrate the Lord's Supper, and in doing so the Christ whose body was given and whose blood was shed will be really present in the Sacrament, a perpetual miracle. In this miracle of the Sacrament the wonders of God's grace in Christ, our Savior, are made real to us. May that blessing be ours! Amen.